1000 great
knitting motifs

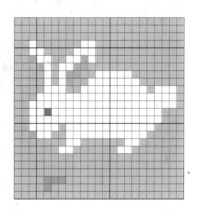

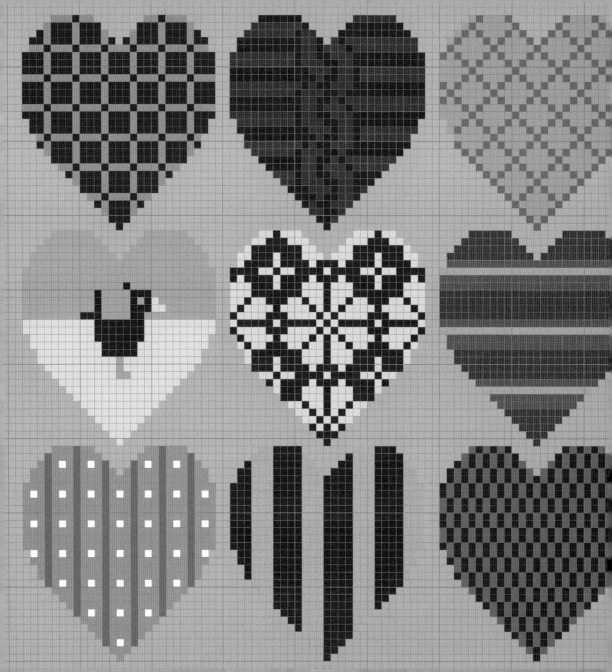

1000 great knitting motifs

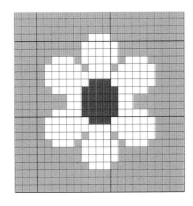

Luise Roberts

Trafalgar Square Publishing

First published in the United States of America in 2004 by
Trafalgar Square Publishing, North Pomfret, Vermont 05053

Reproduction by Annorax Imaging Ltd., UK
Printed and bound by Imago, Thailand

9 8 7 6 5 4 3 2 1

ISBN 1 57076 259 7

Library of Congress Control Number: 2003106325

ILLUSTRATIONS: Kuo Kang Chen
PROJECT EDITOR: Serena Webb

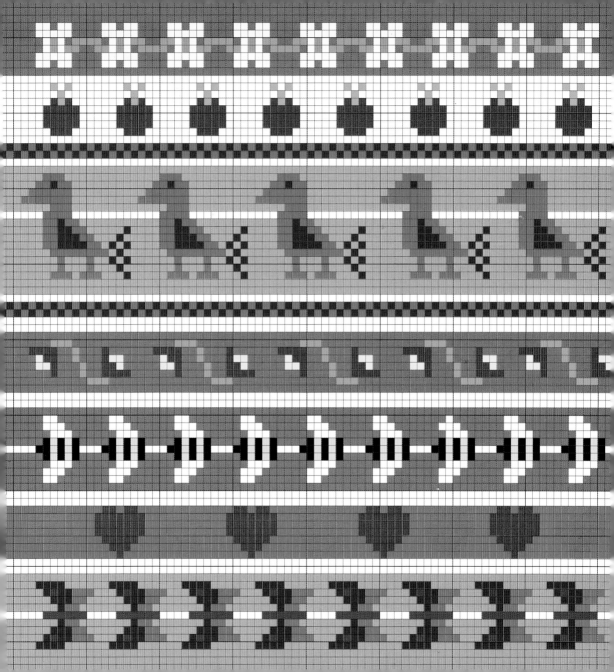

Contents

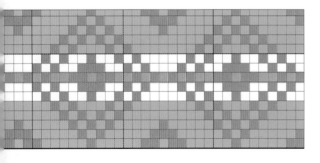

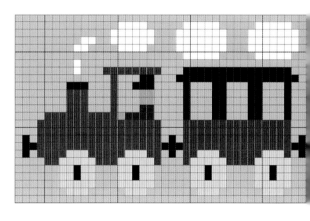

Introduction

Where do you start when deciding what your next knitting project is to be? For me it is the colors of luscious, sweet, smelling yarns; be they cottons, wools or novelty yarns. I love patterns and the interplay color. I love attempting unthinkable combinations and finding that nothing is impossible. However, above all I like to personalize my knitted projects and create something that no one else has in their wardrobe or home. I cannot resist experimenting with adding that little bit extra.

This book is full of those extras that will add something special to a project, whether you are looking for a traditional motif to customize a favorite pattern, a border to edge a plain sweater or a pictorial motif to please a child with a new-found passion for rabbits, trains or flowers. Explore both modern and old motifs in new colors and enjoy the knitting tradition found around the world. Knitting a swatch need never be a trial again! With so many swatches to choose from and so many ways in which you can use them, it should be an exciting adventure.

How to use this book

Each section is ordered by row repeats so designs with one to two row repeats will start a section and larger patterns with larger row repeats will finish a section. Symbols at the top of the page indicate the row repeats on that page. Within similar row repeats the motifs are arranged by horizontal stitch repeats.

Each motif in this book is described by a graph. These follow a standard graph format and show how the pattern would look if viewed from the right side. This allows for use on circular and single pointed needles. The numbers on the right hand side are the row or round numbers. The graph is read from bottom to top and starts at the bottom right with a right side row. If the project is being knitted using single pointed needles then the first stitch on the next row (wrong side) starts one square up from the last stitch on the previous row. For right side rows work from the right to left and for wrong side rows work from the left to right across the graph. If the project is being knitted using circular or double pointed needles then the next row starts on the right again but one square up. This is because when working on circular needles one knits with the right side facing on every row.

The graphs often show more than one repeat to give a better impression of how the motif will look. In such cases, the horizontal repeat is indicated by a thicker vertical rule extending beyond the graph. In cases where there is more than one motif row repeat, the repeat is indicated by a thicker horizontal rule.

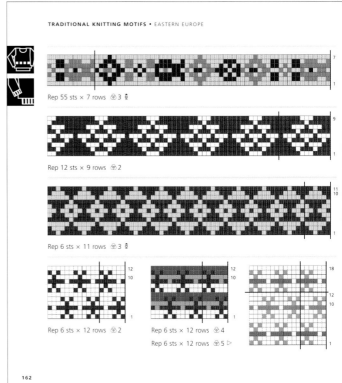

TRADITIONAL KNITTING MOTIFS • EASTERN EUROPE

Rep 55 sts × 7 rows ⊛3 ⦷

Rep 12 sts × 9 rows ⊛2

Rep 6 sts × 11 rows ⊛3 ⦷

Rep 6 sts × 12 rows ⊛2

Rep 6 sts × 12 rows ⊛4

Rep 6 sts × 12 rows ⊛5 ▷

162

Step-by-step guide

1 Starting with a 4in (10cm) gauge (tension) swatch of the chosen yarn and if possible a pattern for the project, estimate the scale of the motif required. This could be a motif with a small row repeat repeated several times, or a single row repeat of a bolder design or perhaps a mixture of the two.

2 Consider the horizontal repeat. It may be necessary to choose a motif that will repeat exactly across the width of the project; remember to allow for an edging stitch on each side (see page 16). This is always a satisfying finish but many traditional Fair Isle garments have a pattern mismatch at the sides or under the arms. If the number of horizontal repeats is seven or under then an odd number of repeats will blend better into the overall scheme. If there are an even number of repeats then the eye will be drawn to the center and divide the pattern and project in to two equal halves.

3 Browse through the sections comparing the designs and key characteristics. Decide a style of motif, find the appropriate row repeat and then consider the possible stitch repeats. Remember the mood of a motif can be changed by the use of a different palette or texture.

4 If a combination of designs are to be used then it is useful to photocopy the possible motifs and try various arrangements. Not only can the order of the motifs or the distance between them change but they can move left and right to vary the pattern alignment.

5 Now for the fun bit. Swatch, and swatch some more until you have a combination of color, texture and motif that would enhance the proposed project.

6 Finally, write out any notes or reminders about the motif that might be forgotten when the project knitting has started and attach the preferred swatch.

Key

Page index

 Motifs suitable for edgings.

 Motifs of fewer than 15 rows.

 Motifs of fewer than 25 rows.

 Motifs of more than 25 rows.

Motif symbols

⊛ Number of colors used including the background color.

⚲ Suitable scale and motif for a child's garment.

Choosing and looking at motifs

Obvious physical constraints, such as the scale and the number of rows will affect your choice of motif, as will its aesthetic properties. There are many ways of looking at a motif to realize its potential.

Color

Choosing colors to use can be quite daunting. A good trick to remember is to put the colors into the basket or onto a table roughly in the proportion they would appear in the project or motif, then assess whether the colors that are to be most prominant are harmonious and that the combinations work together.

The balance of a motif can be altered by swapping the light and dark or the warm and cold shades. Another effective way of influencing the color balance is to use complementary colors. These are colors that appear opposite each other on the color wheel, for instance red and green, blue and orange, purple and yellow and so on around the wheel. If two complementary colors are used in the same quantities they can be very

The balance of a motif (top) can be altered by swapping the lighter and darker tones (second) or the warm and cold tones (third). Motifs in neutral or tones of one color can be highlighted by using a splash of a contrasting color in selected areas (bottom).

distracting, however, if the colors are used in different quantities, or are not exactly complementary, then the effect is of a modern approach to light, dark and contrast. Complementary colors are well worth experimenting with.

Texture

The graphs in this book concentrate on color but many of the motifs work equally well in contrasting textures. This can be created by a combination of knit and purl, raised stitches such as bobbles or loop stitches and by using beads. Another easy alternative is to use contrasting yarns, the obvious being the use of

Using beads, bobbles or textured yarns can be very effective. The graph (left) marks the positions for the bead and bobbles shown in the graph (center). Loop stitch and mohair make an interesting alternative (right).

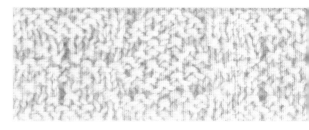

Knit and purl variations can produce some interesting results.

a mohair on a background of worsted (double knitting) yarn.

To work a single color motif in a combination of knit and purl combinations is often a matter of deciding on areas of stockinette (stocking) stitch and reverse stockinette (stocking) stitch. Decide which works best when there are areas of four or more stitches and which gives the motif a structure. For motifs with blocks of ten or more

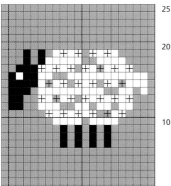

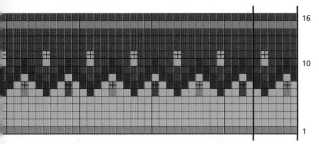

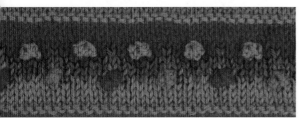

The graph (top) has a cross symbol to indicate a bobble. The swatch is worked in stockinette (stocking) stitch with additional knit rows of row 2 and 16 to create the garter stitch orange stripe.

stitches of solid color, seed (moss) stitch is a good option.

Bobbles and beads always add a bit of fun to a project. Look for motifs with obvious circles of color or accent shapes by themselves, such as at a point or the center of the motif. If beads are positioned by the slip stitch method and are to be used as a block, then it is better to bead every second stitch and every second row. This same arrangement of beads works well for larger bobbles too. Knitting a swatch will help resolve any problems.

Do not forget the delights of using tweeds and chenilles, and yarns such as mohair and boucle, which add a different texture to a project.

Positioning of motifs and edgings

For ideas on where to position motifs look at cloths and furnishing fabrics in stores, at friend's clothes and their homes and at art collections. Use the trends and fashions you see as inspiration for your own ideas.

Motifs
The most important thing to remember is a beautifully knitted motif will draw everyone's attention. Use this to good advantage; position your motif so that the best features are highlighted, this will take the attention away from the areas that are not so good. A single motif on a sweater looks better if it is positioned higher up the chest and used to frame the face. If a motif is too low on a garment it will highlight the hips. If the project is a cushion or an afghan designed to be viewed flat, a single motif will work well centered, or positioned at point two-thirds from an edge.

Edgings or borders
Edgings tend to be long narrow motifs that appear near an edge or at a significant point, such as across the chest or at the center of a project. They tend to draw the eye from an otherwise plain background and give the illusion of extra width. Edgings can be used to unify a project by repeating colors or a section of a main motif. They also add an underline or point of finish to a project.

All over patterns

All the patterns in this book can be repeated as an all over pattern if the project is big enough. They can either be used as a repeat, as indicated by the lines, or they can be offset.

A pattern can be offset in a vertical repeat if half of the repeat is moved to the left or right on the second band of the pattern. The same principle applies for a vertical repeat. Look at wall papers and fabrics and note how single motifs are repeated in a checkered pattern, or as a variation of it, with double spacing in one direction.

Alternate motifs can be reflected so they are facing the other way. However, before considering this variation check that the motif is asymmetrical. To reflect a motif horizontally, so it is facing left rather than right for instance, it is easier to redraw the pattern. However, it is also possible to knit a motif by starting at the bottom left rather than the bottom right. It may be a bit awkward but once the pattern is set it is easy to follow. If the asymmetry exists, a motif can also be reflected top to bottom.

Another variation that can be used for the repeated motif is to rotate it by ninety degrees. However, remember that the height of stockinette (stocking) stitch is approximately seventy percent of its width, so redraw the motif and add an extra row or repeat every third row, to maintain the proportions of the motif.

Whatever your choice, the secret of design in knitting is to always swatch ideas, to keep experimenting and to have fun.

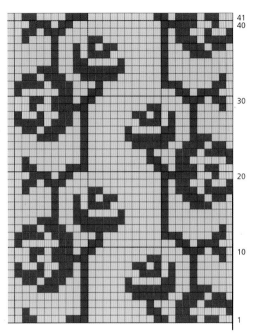

The right repeat has been offset by nine stitches and reflected so that left is now right.

Traditional Fair Isle sweaters

These often have a pattern mismatch at the side of a sweater. This may be due to the difficulty of working in a continuous pattern in the round or because a perfect match would have limited the choice of patterns. Any slight discrepancy in the pattern would be largely hidden by the arms.

Calculating the position and start of stitch pattern repeats

1 Decide on a motif, noting its stitch repeat and if it has a distinct center feature.

2 Calculate or find the number of stitches across a project. Make sure this figure includes any increases or decreases after the cast on stitches and represents the number of stitches at the point at which the motif is to be added.

3 Divide the number of project stitches by the stitch repeat of the pattern.

If the number of stitches left over are only one or two stitches from a full repeat then:
- for one stitch over, check whether or not this can be dropped. If a continuous pattern across a seam is required then consider adding one stitch to the project width to create two seaming stitches. For the right edge, repeat the first repeat stitch twice and for the left edge, repeat the last repeat stitch twice. These extra pattern stitches will fall within the seam.
- for two stitches over, and a project worked on single ended needles, use these stitches as seaming stitch; see above. For a project using circular needles consider working the project with two fewer stitches if there is plenty of ease.
- for one or two stitches under, add the required stitches plus two seaming stitches if required. If these stitches create a significant extra width then decrease the stitches again when it becomes critical to the project, for instance, before the armhole shaping for a sweater or jacket.

If the number of stitches left over after repeating the pattern across the project is more than two stitches from a full repeat then:
- center the motif and create a vertical band of texture or color at the start and end of the pattern repeats and rows. This vertical band will appear as a seam detail or border. To create a significant vertical band that will not look like a mistake consider reducing the number of motif repeats.
- consider adapting the motif. Calculate the number of complete motif repeats. Check if the number of stitches over or under is divisible by the number of motif repeats. If not add the stitches of one full repeat to the calculation. Then either add or remove one stitch from each motif or every second motif. In general, adding a stitch to the center or to the end of the motif repeat works best.

4 Look at the motif again and decide where in the repeat the first stitch will be. It can be the first stitch to the right of the right repeat rule, or it can be anywhere between the two rules. If the motif repeat is large with a distinct center, then consider aligning it with the center of the project.

5 Make a note of your calculations and the logic behind your decisions before proceeding to knit. It is surprising how easy it is to forget.

Traditional knitting motifs

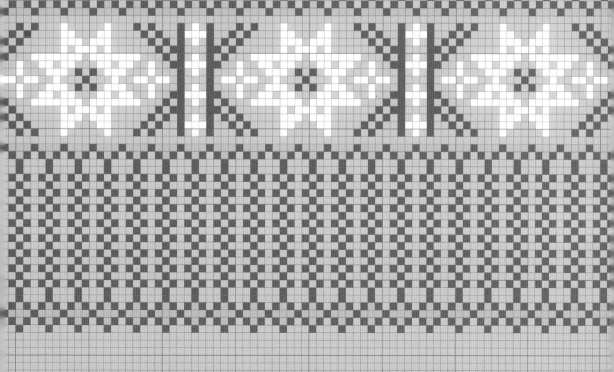

Fair Isle

Fair Isle is the traditional knitting style of the Shetland Islands, found off the northern tip of Scotland. Heavily influenced by traders and invaders from Northern Europe, the traditonal knitting designs have in turn influenced other cultures who have adapted them to suit their color pallette and style. The key feature of a traditional Fair Isle garment is the use of bands of motifs, usually alternate one to four row repeats with deeper row repeats. Originally the colors used were limited to those of natural dyes and wools however synthetic dyes appeared in the mid 1800s.

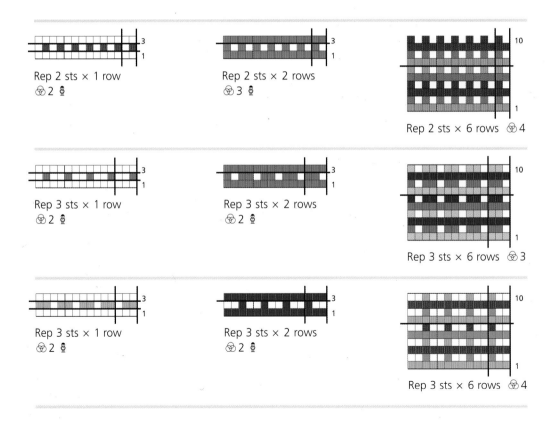

Rep 2 sts × 1 row
⊛ 2 ▯

Rep 2 sts × 2 rows
⊛ 3 ▯

Rep 2 sts × 6 rows   ⊛ 4

Rep 3 sts × 1 row
⊛ 2 ▯

Rep 3 sts × 2 rows
⊛ 2 ▯

Rep 3 sts × 6 rows   ⊛ 3

Rep 3 sts × 1 row
⊛ 2 ▯

Rep 3 sts × 2 rows
⊛ 2 ▯

Rep 3 sts × 6 rows   ⊛ 4

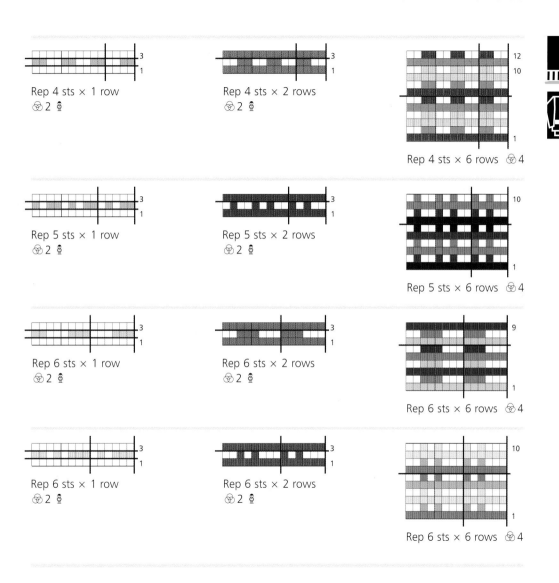

Rep 4 sts × 1 row
⊗2 ⊗

Rep 4 sts × 2 rows
⊗2 ⊗

Rep 4 sts × 6 rows ⊗4

Rep 5 sts × 1 row
⊗2 ⊗

Rep 5 sts × 2 rows
⊗2 ⊗

Rep 5 sts × 6 rows ⊗4

Rep 6 sts × 1 row
⊗2 ⊗

Rep 6 sts × 2 rows
⊗2 ⊗

Rep 6 sts × 6 rows ⊗4

Rep 6 sts × 1 row
⊗2 ⊗

Rep 6 sts × 2 rows
⊗2 ⊗

Rep 6 sts × 6 rows ⊗4

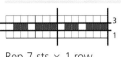

Rep 7 sts × 1 row
🌀2 👤

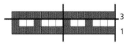

Rep 7 sts × 2 rows
🌀2 👤

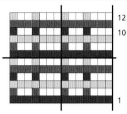

Rep 7 sts × 6 rows 🌀4

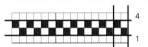

Rep 2 sts × 2 rows
🌀2 👤

Rep 2 sts × 4 rows
🌀3 👤

Rep 2 sts × 3 rows
🌀3 👤

Rep 3 sts × 2 rows 🌀2 👤

Rep 3 sts × 2 rows 🌀3 👤

Rep 4 sts × 2 rows 🌀2 👤

Rep 4 sts × 2 rows 🌀2 👤

Rep 4 sts × 2 rows 🌀3 👤

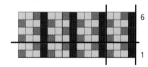

Rep 4 sts × 2 rows 🌀3

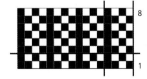

Rep 4 sts × 2 rows 🌀2 👤

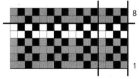

Rep 4 sts × 6 rows 🌀3 👤

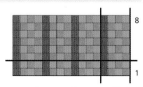

Rep 4 sts × 2 rows 🌀3 👤

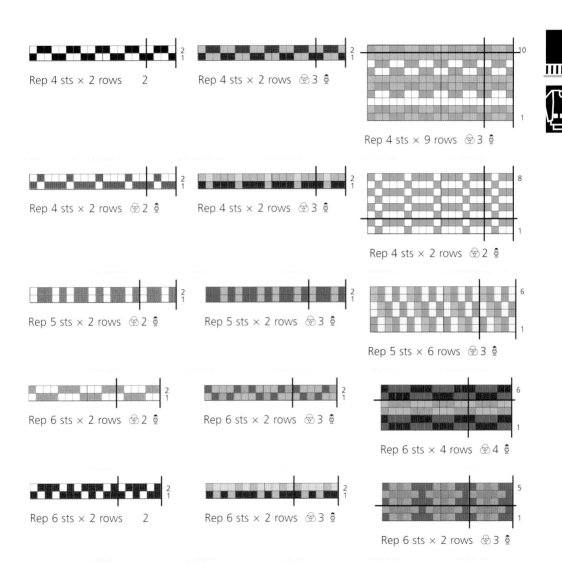

Rep 4 sts × 2 rows   2

Rep 4 sts × 2 rows ✾3 ☗

Rep 4 sts × 9 rows ✾3 ☗

Rep 4 sts × 2 rows ✾2 ☗

Rep 4 sts × 2 rows ✾3 ☗

Rep 4 sts × 2 rows ✾2 ☗

Rep 5 sts × 2 rows ✾2 ☗

Rep 5 sts × 2 rows ✾3 ☗

Rep 5 sts × 6 rows ✾3 ☗

Rep 6 sts × 2 rows ✾2 ☗

Rep 6 sts × 2 rows ✾3 ☗

Rep 6 sts × 4 rows ✾4 ☗

Rep 6 sts × 2 rows   2

Rep 6 sts × 2 rows ✾3 ☗

Rep 6 sts × 2 rows ✾3 ☗

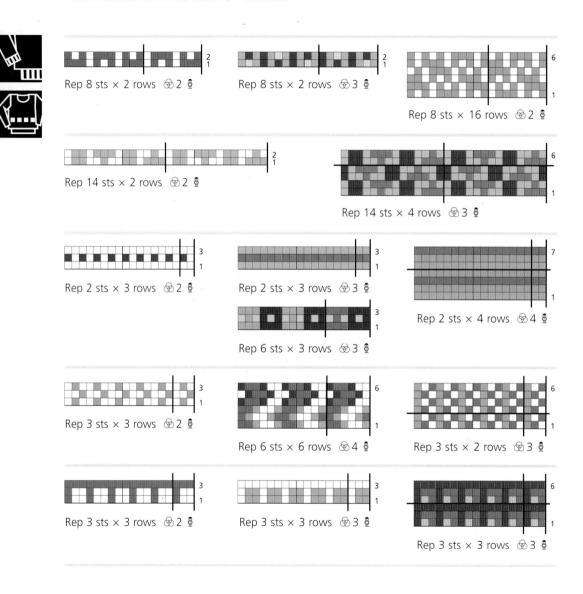

Rep 8 sts × 2 rows ⊛2 ⚇

Rep 8 sts × 2 rows ⊛3 ⚇

Rep 8 sts × 16 rows ⊛2 ⚇

Rep 14 sts × 2 rows ⊛2 ⚇

Rep 14 sts × 4 rows ⊛3 ⚇

Rep 2 sts × 3 rows ⊛2 ⚇

Rep 2 sts × 3 rows ⊛3 ⚇

Rep 2 sts × 4 rows ⊛4 ⚇

Rep 6 sts × 3 rows ⊛3 ⚇

Rep 3 sts × 3 rows ⊛2 ⚇

Rep 6 sts × 6 rows ⊛4 ⚇

Rep 3 sts × 2 rows ⊛3 ⚇

Rep 3 sts × 3 rows ⊛2 ⚇

Rep 3 sts × 3 rows ⊛3 ⚇

Rep 3 sts × 3 rows ⊛3 ⚇

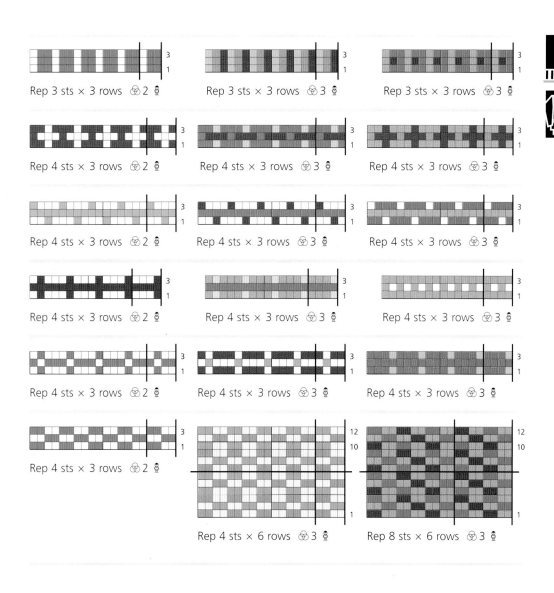

Rep 3 sts × 3 rows ⊛2 ⚇

Rep 3 sts × 3 rows ⊛3 ⚇

Rep 3 sts × 3 rows ⊛3 ⚇

Rep 4 sts × 3 rows ⊛2 ⚇

Rep 4 sts × 3 rows ⊛3 ⚇

Rep 4 sts × 3 rows ⊛3 ⚇

Rep 4 sts × 3 rows ⊛2 ⚇

Rep 4 sts × 3 rows ⊛3 ⚇

Rep 4 sts × 3 rows ⊛3 ⚇

Rep 4 sts × 3 rows ⊛2 ⚇

Rep 4 sts × 3 rows ⊛3 ⚇

Rep 4 sts × 3 rows ⊛3 ⚇

Rep 4 sts × 3 rows ⊛2 ⚇

Rep 4 sts × 3 rows ⊛3 ⚇

Rep 4 sts × 3 rows ⊛3 ⚇

Rep 4 sts × 3 rows ⊛2 ⚇

Rep 4 sts × 6 rows ⊛3 ⚇

Rep 8 sts × 6 rows ⊛3 ⚇

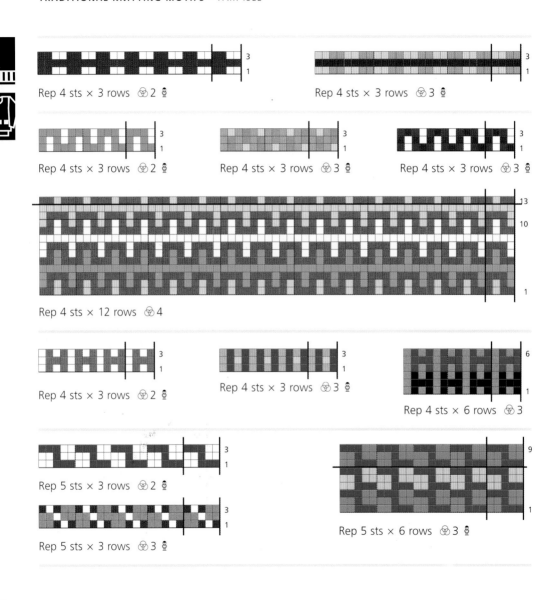

Rep 4 sts × 3 rows ⊛2 🯅

Rep 4 sts × 3 rows ⊛3 🯅

Rep 4 sts × 3 rows ⊛2 🯅

Rep 4 sts × 3 rows ⊛3 🯅

Rep 4 sts × 3 rows ⊛3 🯅

Rep 4 sts × 12 rows ⊛4

Rep 4 sts × 3 rows ⊛2 🯅

Rep 4 sts × 3 rows ⊛3 🯅

Rep 4 sts × 6 rows ⊛3

Rep 5 sts × 3 rows ⊛2 🯅

Rep 5 sts × 6 rows ⊛3 🯅

Rep 5 sts × 3 rows ⊛3 🯅

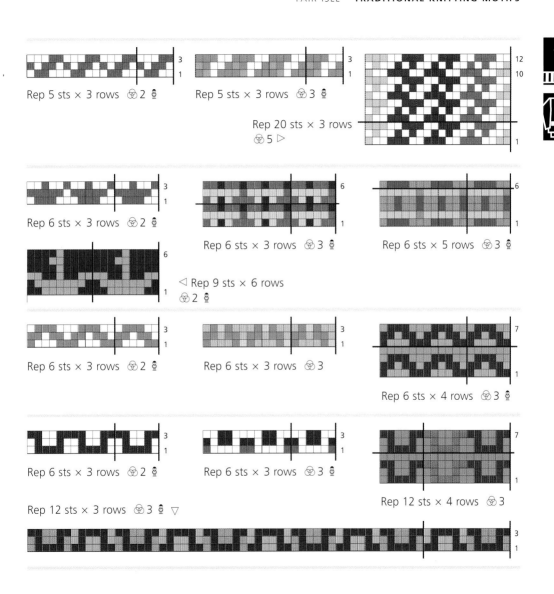

Rep 5 sts × 3 rows ⊗2 ☗

Rep 5 sts × 3 rows ⊗3 ☗

Rep 20 sts × 3 rows
⊗5 ▷

Rep 6 sts × 3 rows ⊗2 ☗

Rep 6 sts × 3 rows ⊗3 ☗

Rep 6 sts × 5 rows ⊗3 ☗

◁ Rep 9 sts × 6 rows
⊗2 ☗

Rep 6 sts × 3 rows ⊗2 ☗

Rep 6 sts × 3 rows ⊗3

Rep 6 sts × 4 rows ⊗3 ☗

Rep 6 sts × 3 rows ⊗2 ☗

Rep 6 sts × 3 rows ⊗3 ☗

Rep 12 sts × 4 rows ⊗3

Rep 12 sts × 3 rows ⊗3 ☗ ▽

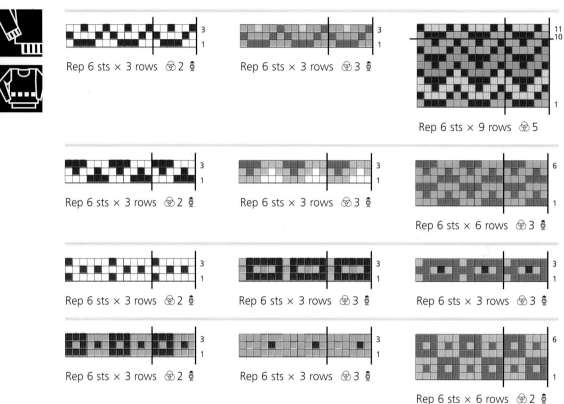

Rep 6 sts × 3 rows ⊛ 2 🎅

Rep 6 sts × 3 rows ⊛ 3 🎅

Rep 6 sts × 9 rows ⊛ 5

Rep 6 sts × 3 rows ⊛ 2 🎅

Rep 6 sts × 3 rows ⊛ 3 🎅

Rep 6 sts × 6 rows ⊛ 3 🎅

Rep 6 sts × 3 rows ⊛ 2 🎅

Rep 6 sts × 3 rows ⊛ 3 🎅

Rep 6 sts × 3 rows ⊛ 3 🎅

Rep 6 sts × 3 rows ⊛ 2 🎅

Rep 6 sts × 3 rows ⊛ 3 🎅

Rep 6 sts × 6 rows ⊛ 2 🎅

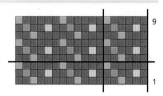

Rep 6 sts × 3 rows ⊛ 2 🎅

Rep 6 sts × 3 rows ⊛ 3

Rep 6 sts × 3 rows ⊛ 4 🎅

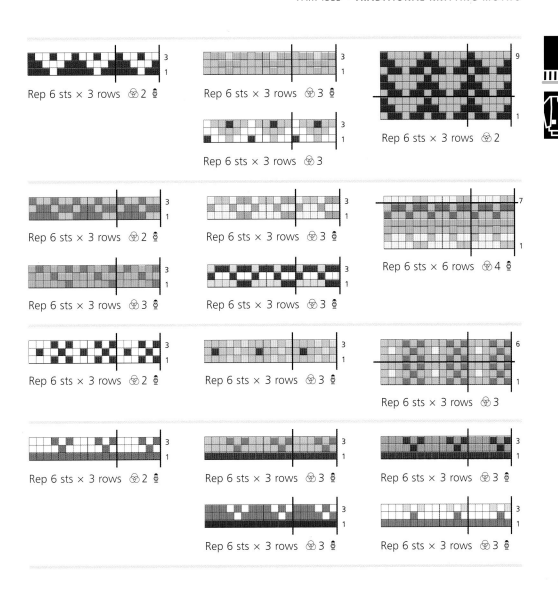

Rep 6 sts × 3 rows ⊛2 🧍

Rep 6 sts × 3 rows ⊛3 🧍

Rep 6 sts × 3 rows ⊛3

Rep 6 sts × 3 rows ⊛2

Rep 6 sts × 3 rows ⊛2 🧍

Rep 6 sts × 3 rows ⊛3 🧍

Rep 6 sts × 3 rows ⊛3 🧍

Rep 6 sts × 3 rows ⊛3 🧍

Rep 6 sts × 6 rows ⊛4 🧍

Rep 6 sts × 3 rows ⊛2 🧍

Rep 6 sts × 3 rows ⊛3 🧍

Rep 6 sts × 3 rows ⊛3

Rep 6 sts × 3 rows ⊛2 🧍

Rep 6 sts × 3 rows ⊛3 🧍

Rep 6 sts × 3 rows ⊛3 🧍

Rep 6 sts × 3 rows ⊛3 🧍

Rep 6 sts × 3 rows ⊛3 🧍

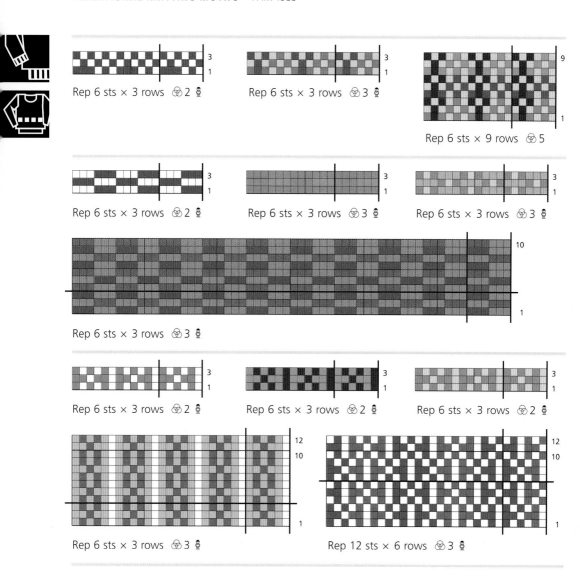

Rep 6 sts × 3 rows ⊛2 🕯

Rep 6 sts × 3 rows ⊛3 🕯

Rep 6 sts × 9 rows ⊛5

Rep 6 sts × 3 rows ⊛2 🕯

Rep 6 sts × 3 rows ⊛3 🕯

Rep 6 sts × 3 rows ⊛3 🕯

Rep 6 sts × 3 rows ⊛3 🕯

Rep 6 sts × 3 rows ⊛2 🕯

Rep 6 sts × 3 rows ⊛2 🕯

Rep 6 sts × 3 rows ⊛2 🕯

Rep 6 sts × 3 rows ⊛3 🕯

Rep 12 sts × 6 rows ⊛3 🕯

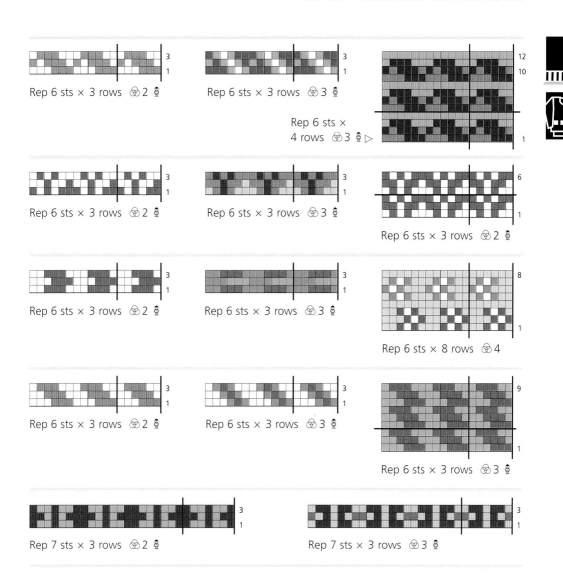

Rep 6 sts × 3 rows ⊛2 🕯

Rep 6 sts × 3 rows ⊛3 🕯

Rep 6 sts ×
4 rows ⊛3 🕯 ▷

Rep 6 sts × 3 rows ⊛2 🕯

Rep 6 sts × 3 rows ⊛3 🕯

Rep 6 sts × 3 rows ⊛2 🕯

Rep 6 sts × 3 rows ⊛2 🕯

Rep 6 sts × 3 rows ⊛3 🕯

Rep 6 sts × 8 rows ⊛4

Rep 6 sts × 3 rows ⊛2 🕯

Rep 6 sts × 3 rows ⊛3 🕯

Rep 6 sts × 3 rows ⊛3 🕯

Rep 7 sts × 3 rows ⊛2 🕯

Rep 7 sts × 3 rows ⊛3 🕯

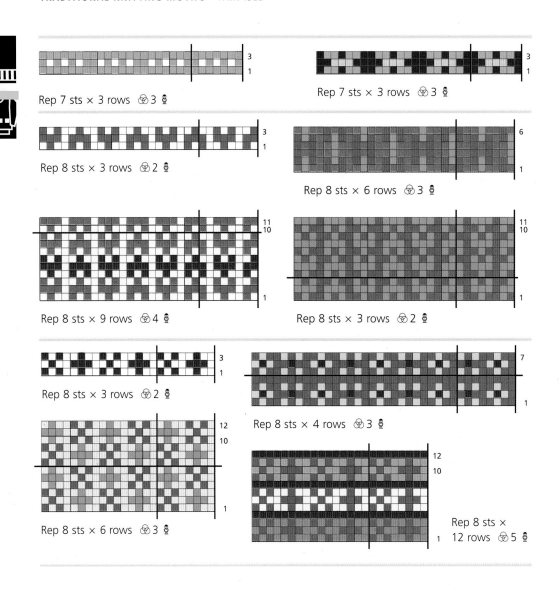

Rep 7 sts × 3 rows ⊛ 3 ⚇

Rep 7 sts × 3 rows ⊛ 3 ⚇

Rep 8 sts × 3 rows ⊛ 2 ⚇

Rep 8 sts × 6 rows ⊛ 3 ⚇

Rep 8 sts × 9 rows ⊛ 4 ⚇

Rep 8 sts × 3 rows ⊛ 2 ⚇

Rep 8 sts × 3 rows ⊛ 2 ⚇

Rep 8 sts × 4 rows ⊛ 3 ⚇

Rep 8 sts × 6 rows ⊛ 3 ⚇

Rep 8 sts × 12 rows ⊛ 5 ⚇

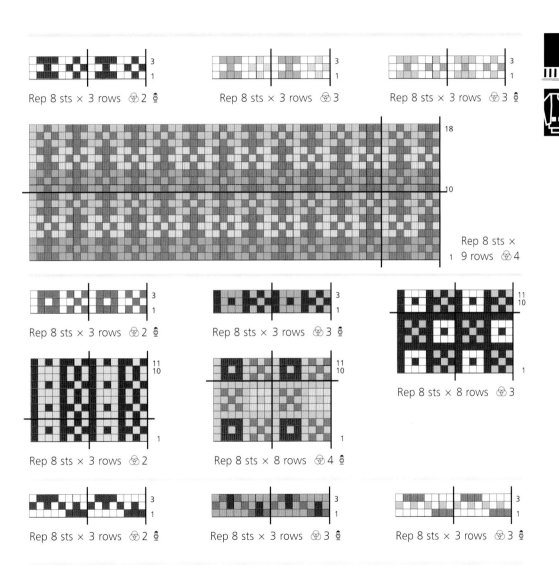

Rep 8 sts × 3 rows ⊛2 ⏚

Rep 8 sts × 3 rows ⊛3

Rep 8 sts × 3 rows ⊛3 ⏚

Rep 8 sts × 9 rows ⊛4

Rep 8 sts × 3 rows ⊛2 ⏚

Rep 8 sts × 3 rows ⊛3 ⏚

Rep 8 sts × 8 rows ⊛3

Rep 8 sts × 3 rows ⊛2

Rep 8 sts × 8 rows ⊛4 ⏚

Rep 8 sts × 3 rows ⊛2 ⏚

Rep 8 sts × 3 rows ⊛3 ⏚

Rep 8 sts × 3 rows ⊛3 ⏚

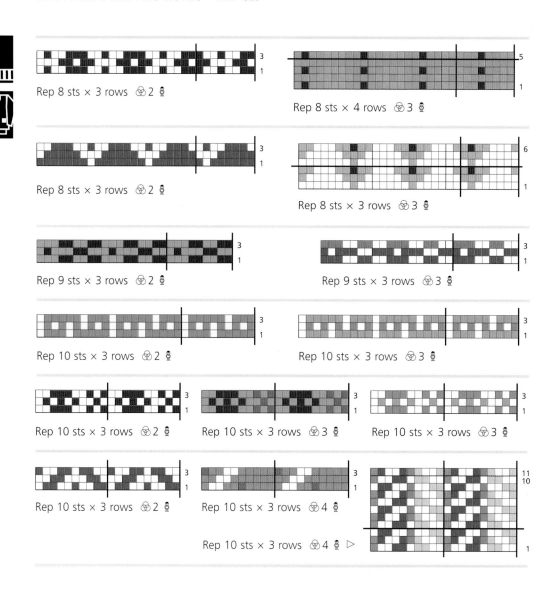

Rep 8 sts × 3 rows ⊛2 🕯

Rep 8 sts × 4 rows ⊛3 🕯

Rep 8 sts × 3 rows ⊛2 🕯

Rep 8 sts × 3 rows ⊛3 🕯

Rep 9 sts × 3 rows ⊛2 🕯

Rep 9 sts × 3 rows ⊛3 🕯

Rep 10 sts × 3 rows ⊛2 🕯

Rep 10 sts × 3 rows ⊛3 🕯

Rep 10 sts × 3 rows ⊛2 🕯

Rep 10 sts × 3 rows ⊛3 🕯

Rep 10 sts × 3 rows ⊛3 🕯

Rep 10 sts × 3 rows ⊛2 🕯

Rep 10 sts × 3 rows ⊛4 🕯

Rep 10 sts × 3 rows ⊛4 🕯 ▷

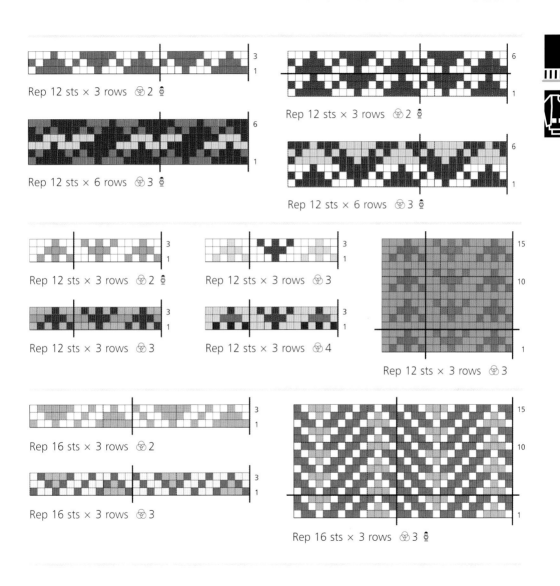

Rep 12 sts × 3 rows ⊛ 2 ⚱

Rep 12 sts × 6 rows ⊛ 3 ⚱

Rep 12 sts × 3 rows ⊛ 2 ⚱

Rep 12 sts × 6 rows ⊛ 3 ⚱

Rep 12 sts × 3 rows ⊛ 2 ⚱

Rep 12 sts × 3 rows ⊛ 3

Rep 12 sts × 3 rows ⊛ 3

Rep 12 sts × 3 rows ⊛ 4

Rep 12 sts × 3 rows ⊛ 3

Rep 16 sts × 3 rows ⊛ 2

Rep 16 sts × 3 rows ⊛ 3

Rep 16 sts × 3 rows ⊛ 3 ⚱

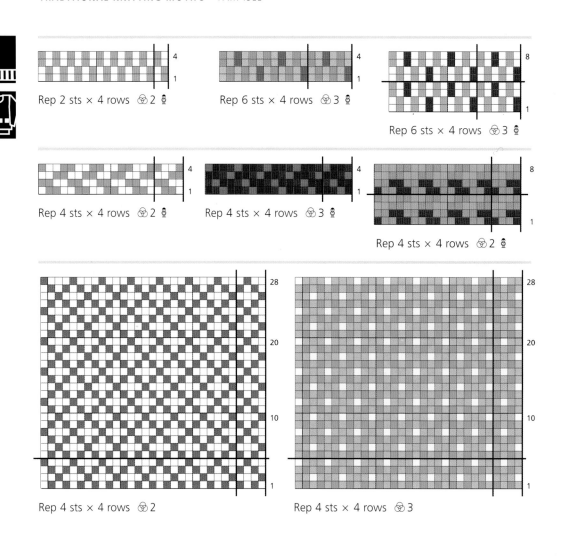

Rep 2 sts × 4 rows ⊛2 ⌘

Rep 6 sts × 4 rows ⊛3 ⌘

Rep 6 sts × 4 rows ⊛3 ⌘

Rep 4 sts × 4 rows ⊛2 ⌘

Rep 4 sts × 4 rows ⊛3 ⌘

Rep 4 sts × 4 rows ⊛2 ⌘

Rep 4 sts × 4 rows ⊛2

Rep 4 sts × 4 rows ⊛3

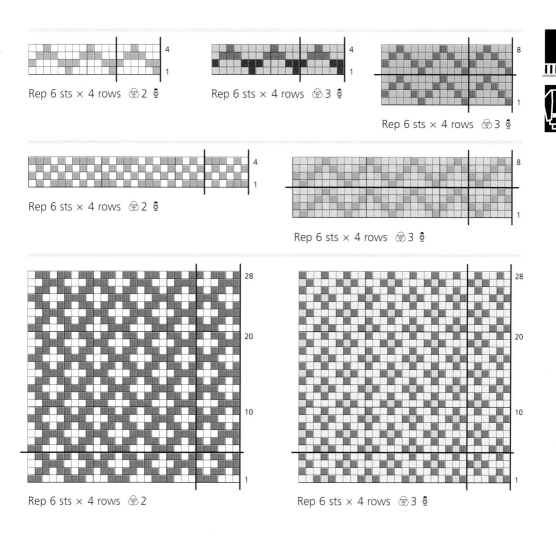

Rep 6 sts × 4 rows ⊛2 ⸙

Rep 6 sts × 4 rows ⊛3 ⸙

Rep 6 sts × 4 rows ⊛3 ⸙

Rep 6 sts × 4 rows ⊛2 ⸙

Rep 6 sts × 4 rows ⊛3 ⸙

Rep 6 sts × 4 rows ⊛2

Rep 6 sts × 4 rows ⊛3 ⸙

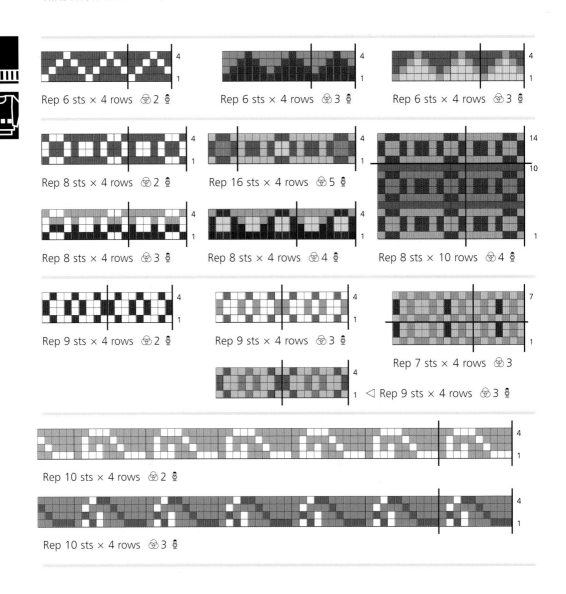

Rep 6 sts × 4 rows ⊛ 2 ⸙

Rep 6 sts × 4 rows ⊛ 3 ⸙

Rep 6 sts × 4 rows ⊛ 3 ⸙

Rep 8 sts × 4 rows ⊛ 2 ⸙

Rep 16 sts × 4 rows ⊛ 5 ⸙

Rep 8 sts × 4 rows ⊛ 3 ⸙

Rep 8 sts × 4 rows ⊛ 4 ⸙

Rep 8 sts × 10 rows ⊛ 4 ⸙

Rep 9 sts × 4 rows ⊛ 2 ⸙

Rep 9 sts × 4 rows ⊛ 3 ⸙

Rep 7 sts × 4 rows ⊛ 3

◁ Rep 9 sts × 4 rows ⊛ 3 ⸙

Rep 10 sts × 4 rows ⊛ 2 ⸙

Rep 10 sts × 4 rows ⊛ 3 ⸙

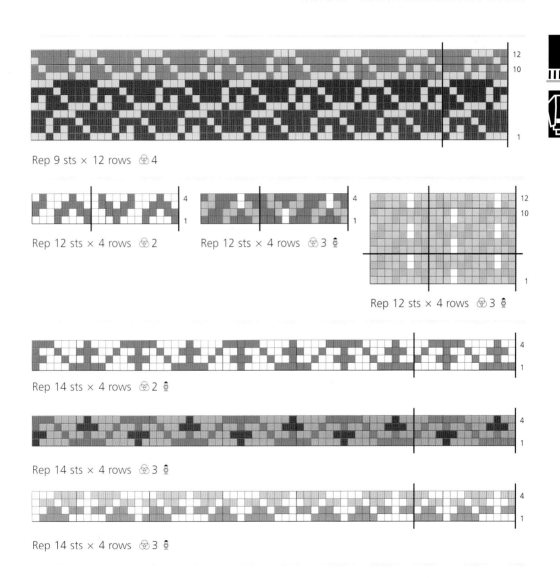

Rep 9 sts × 12 rows ⊛ 4

Rep 12 sts × 4 rows ⊛ 2

Rep 12 sts × 4 rows ⊛ 3 ♟

Rep 12 sts × 4 rows ⊛ 3 ♟

Rep 14 sts × 4 rows ⊛ 2 ♟

Rep 14 sts × 4 rows ⊛ 3 ♟

Rep 14 sts × 4 rows ⊛ 3 ♟

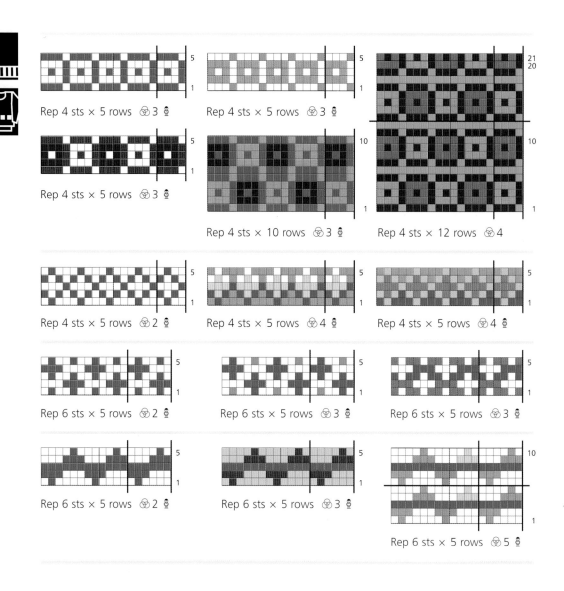

Rep 4 sts × 5 rows ✪3 ☗

Rep 4 sts × 5 rows ✪3 ☗

Rep 4 sts × 5 rows ✪3 ☗

Rep 4 sts × 10 rows ✪3 ☗

Rep 4 sts × 12 rows ✪4

Rep 4 sts × 5 rows ✪2 ☗

Rep 4 sts × 5 rows ✪4 ☗

Rep 4 sts × 5 rows ✪4 ☗

Rep 6 sts × 5 rows ✪2 ☗

Rep 6 sts × 5 rows ✪3 ☗

Rep 6 sts × 5 rows ✪3 ☗

Rep 6 sts × 5 rows ✪2 ☗

Rep 6 sts × 5 rows ✪3 ☗

Rep 6 sts × 5 rows ✪5 ☗

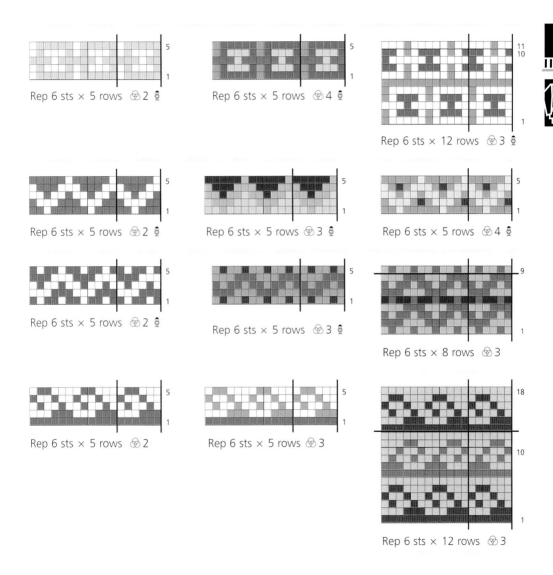

Rep 6 sts × 5 rows ✿2

Rep 6 sts × 5 rows ✿4

Rep 6 sts × 12 rows ✿3

Rep 6 sts × 5 rows ✿2

Rep 6 sts × 5 rows ✿3

Rep 6 sts × 5 rows ✿4

Rep 6 sts × 5 rows ✿2

Rep 6 sts × 5 rows ✿3

Rep 6 sts × 8 rows ✿3

Rep 6 sts × 5 rows ✿2

Rep 6 sts × 5 rows ✿3

Rep 6 sts × 12 rows ✿3

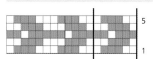

Rep 6 sts × 5 rows ⊕2 🎅

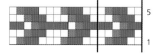

Rep 6 sts × 5 rows ⊕3

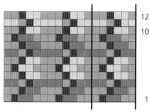

Rep 6 sts × 12 rows ⊕4

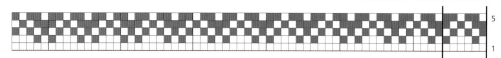

Rep 6 sts × 5 rows ⊕2 🎅

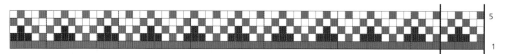

Rep 6 sts × 5 rows ⊕3 🎅

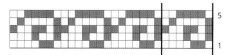

Rep 7 sts × 5 rows ⊕2 🎅

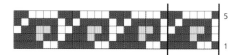

7 sts × 5 rows ⊕3 🎅

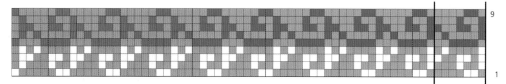

Rep 7 sts × 9 rows ⊕3 🎅

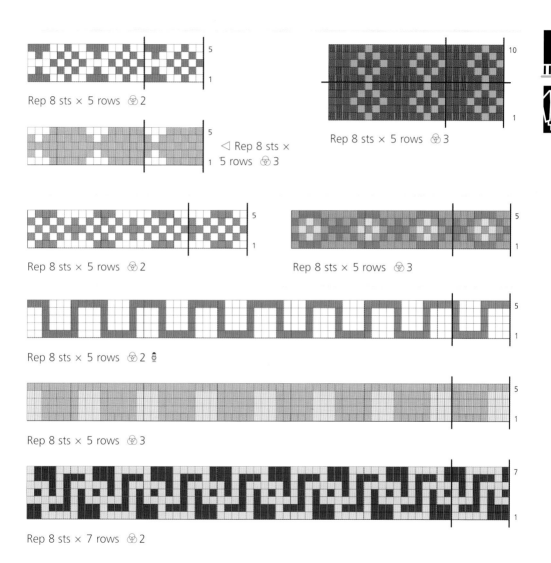

Rep 8 sts × 5 rows ⊛ 2

◁ Rep 8 sts × 5 rows ⊛ 3

Rep 8 sts × 5 rows ⊛ 3

Rep 8 sts × 5 rows ⊛ 2

Rep 8 sts × 5 rows ⊛ 3

Rep 8 sts × 5 rows ⊛ 2 ⓰

Rep 8 sts × 5 rows ⊛ 3

Rep 8 sts × 7 rows ⊛ 2

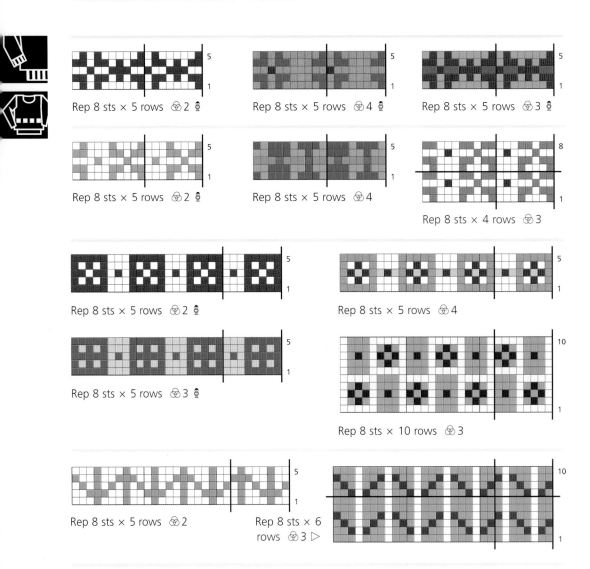

Rep 8 sts × 5 rows ⊛2 👤

Rep 8 sts × 5 rows ⊛4 👤

Rep 8 sts × 5 rows ⊛3 👤

Rep 8 sts × 5 rows ⊛2 👤

Rep 8 sts × 5 rows ⊛4

Rep 8 sts × 4 rows ⊛3

Rep 8 sts × 5 rows ⊛2 👤

Rep 8 sts × 5 rows ⊛4

Rep 8 sts × 5 rows ⊛3 👤

Rep 8 sts × 10 rows ⊛3

Rep 8 sts × 5 rows ⊛2

Rep 8 sts × 6 rows ⊛3 ▷

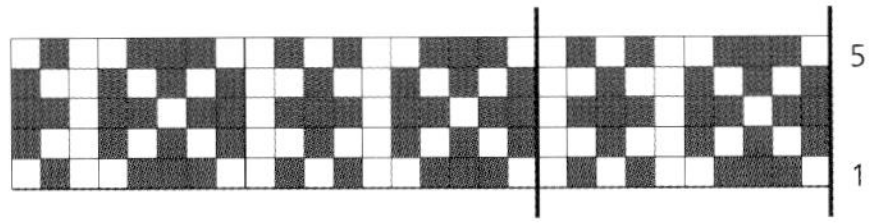

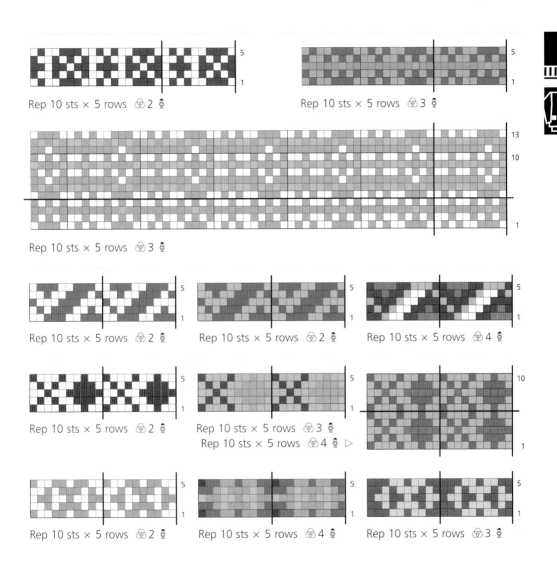

Rep 10 sts × 5 rows 2

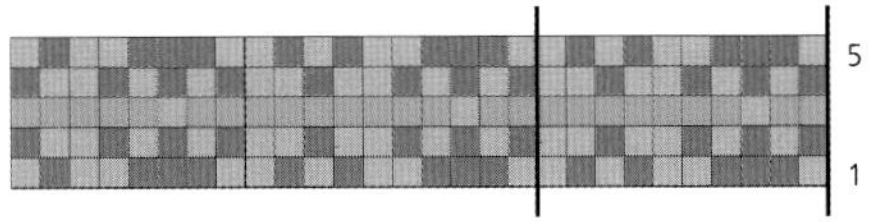

Rep 10 sts × 5 rows 3

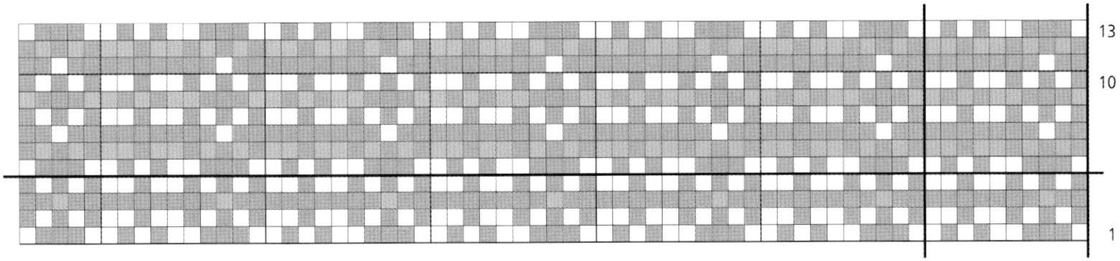

Rep 10 sts × 5 rows 3

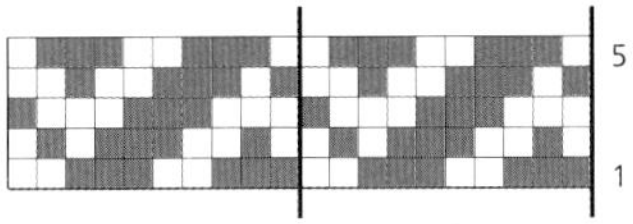

Rep 10 sts × 5 rows 2

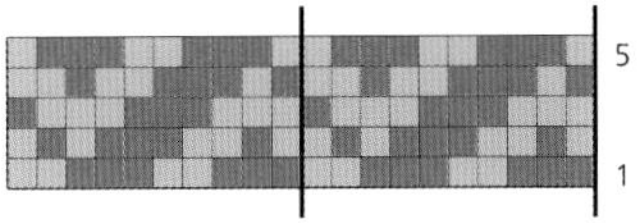

Rep 10 sts × 5 rows 2

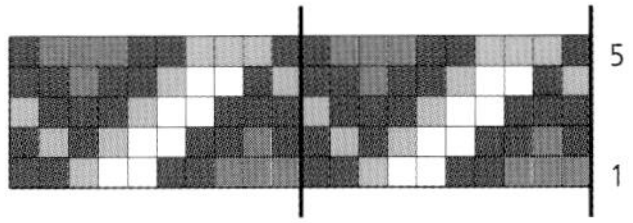

Rep 10 sts × 5 rows 4

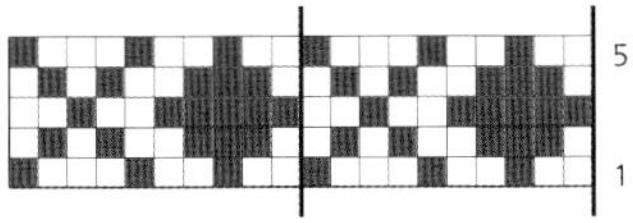

Rep 10 sts × 5 rows 2

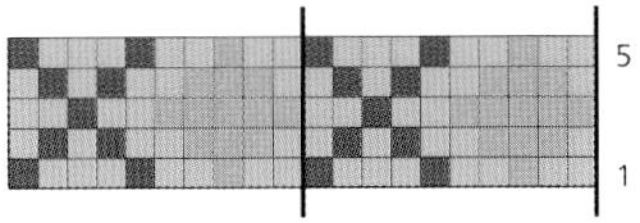

Rep 10 sts × 5 rows 3

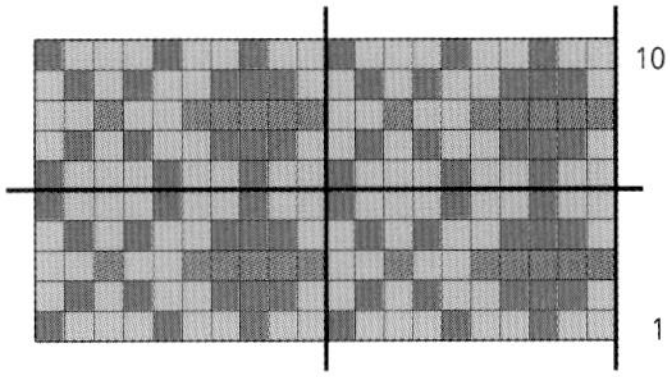

Rep 10 sts × 5 rows 4 ▷

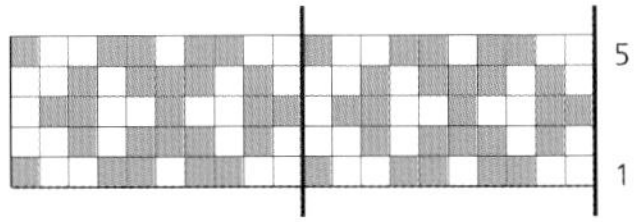

Rep 10 sts × 5 rows 2

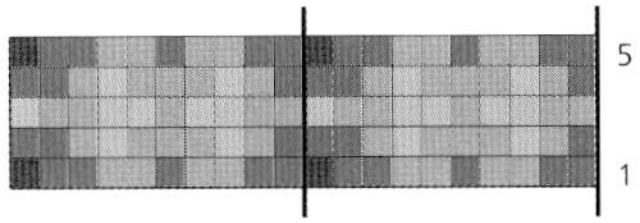

Rep 10 sts × 5 rows 4

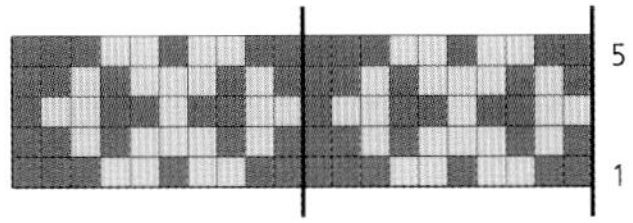

Rep 10 sts × 5 rows 3

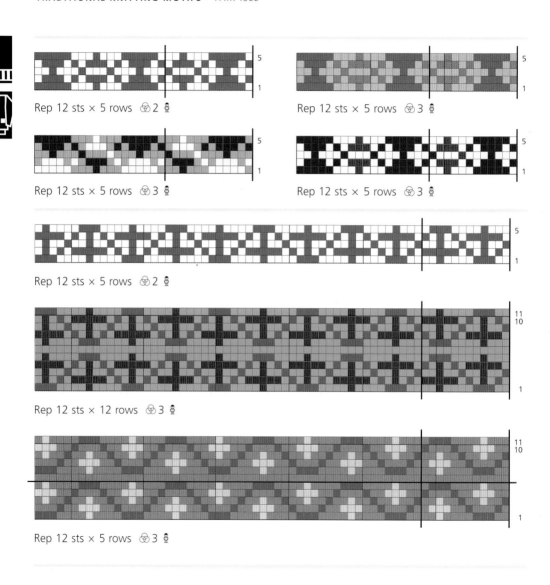

Rep 12 sts × 5 rows ⊗2 ⚇

Rep 12 sts × 5 rows ⊗3 ⚇

Rep 12 sts × 5 rows ⊗3 ⚇

Rep 12 sts × 5 rows ⊗3 ⚇

Rep 12 sts × 5 rows ⊗2 ⚇

Rep 12 sts × 12 rows ⊗3 ⚇

Rep 12 sts × 5 rows ⊗3 ⚇

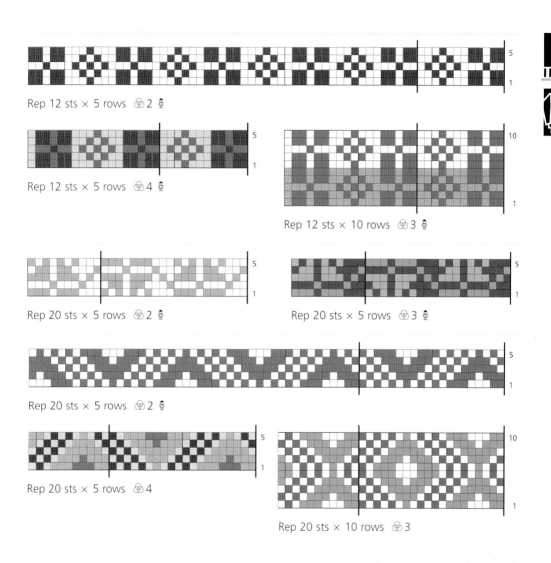

Rep 12 sts × 5 rows ⊛ 2 🎎

Rep 12 sts × 5 rows ⊛ 4 🎎

Rep 12 sts × 10 rows ⊛ 3 🎎

Rep 20 sts × 5 rows ⊛ 2 🎎

Rep 20 sts × 5 rows ⊛ 3 🎎

Rep 20 sts × 5 rows ⊛ 2 🎎

Rep 20 sts × 5 rows ⊛ 4

Rep 20 sts × 10 rows ⊛ 3

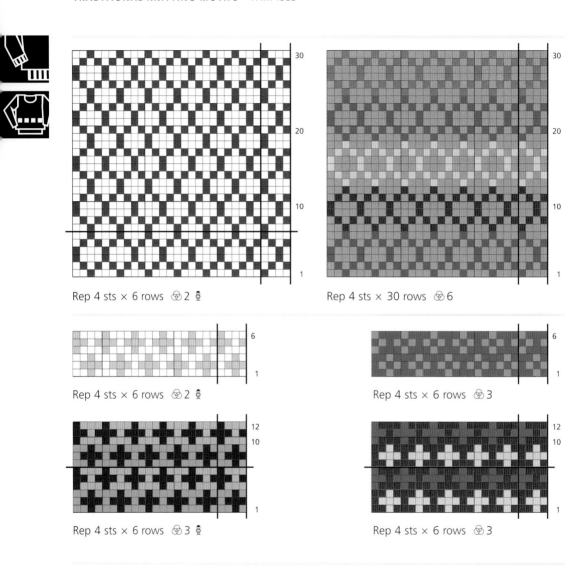

Rep 4 sts × 6 rows ⊗ 2 ⚇

Rep 4 sts × 30 rows ⊗ 6

Rep 4 sts × 6 rows ⊗ 2 ⚇

Rep 4 sts × 6 rows ⊗ 3

Rep 4 sts × 6 rows ⊗ 3 ⚇

Rep 4 sts × 6 rows ⊗ 3

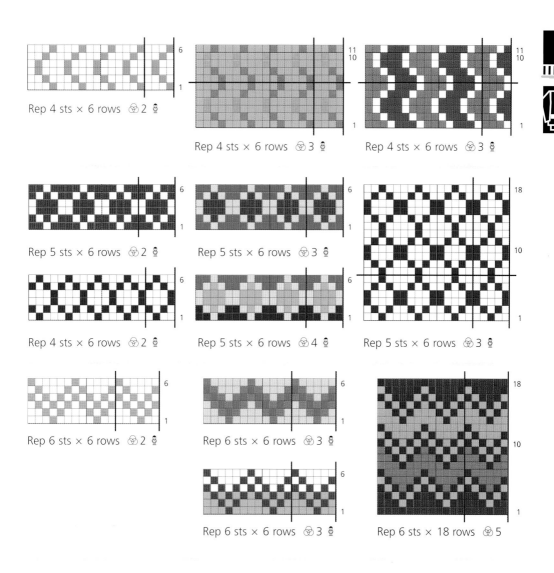

Rep 4 sts × 6 rows ⊛2 ⬤

Rep 4 sts × 6 rows ⊛3 ⬤

Rep 4 sts × 6 rows ⊛3 ⬤

Rep 5 sts × 6 rows ⊛2 ⬤

Rep 5 sts × 6 rows ⊛3 ⬤

Rep 5 sts × 6 rows ⊛3 ⬤

Rep 4 sts × 6 rows ⊛2 ⬤

Rep 5 sts × 6 rows ⊛4 ⬤

Rep 6 sts × 6 rows ⊛2 ⬤

Rep 6 sts × 6 rows ⊛3 ⬤

Rep 6 sts × 18 rows ⊛5

Rep 6 sts × 6 rows ⊛3 ⬤

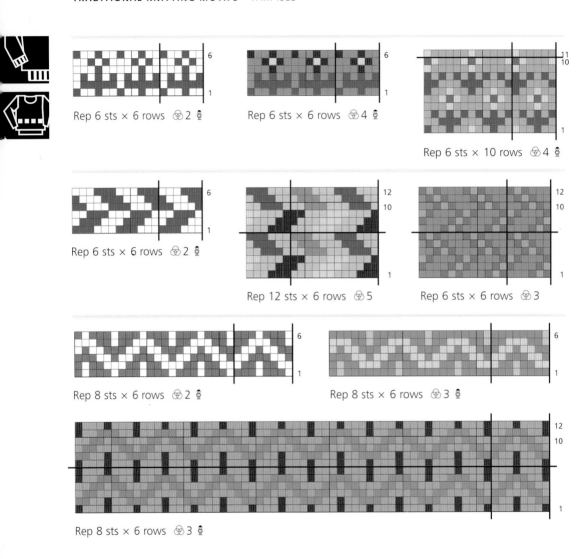

Rep 6 sts × 6 rows ⊛2

Rep 6 sts × 6 rows ⊛4

Rep 6 sts × 10 rows ⊛4

Rep 6 sts × 6 rows ⊛2

Rep 12 sts × 6 rows ⊛5

Rep 6 sts × 6 rows ⊛3

Rep 8 sts × 6 rows ⊛2

Rep 8 sts × 6 rows ⊛3

Rep 8 sts × 6 rows ⊛3

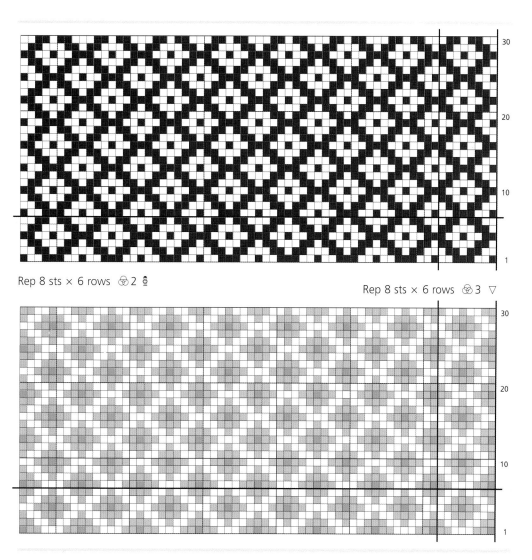

Rep 8 sts × 6 rows ⊛2 ⚇   Rep 8 sts × 6 rows ⊛3 ▽

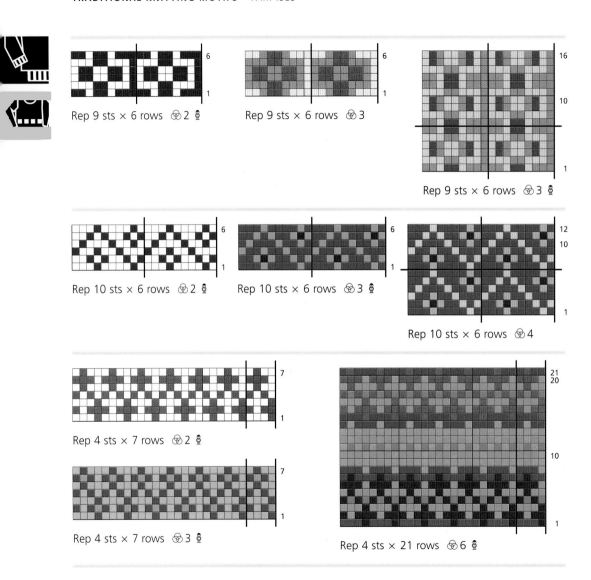

Rep 9 sts × 6 rows ⊛ 2

Rep 9 sts × 6 rows ⊛ 3

Rep 9 sts × 6 rows ⊛ 3

Rep 10 sts × 6 rows ⊛ 2

Rep 10 sts × 6 rows ⊛ 3

Rep 10 sts × 6 rows ⊛ 4

Rep 4 sts × 7 rows ⊛ 2

Rep 4 sts × 7 rows ⊛ 3

Rep 4 sts × 21 rows ⊛ 6

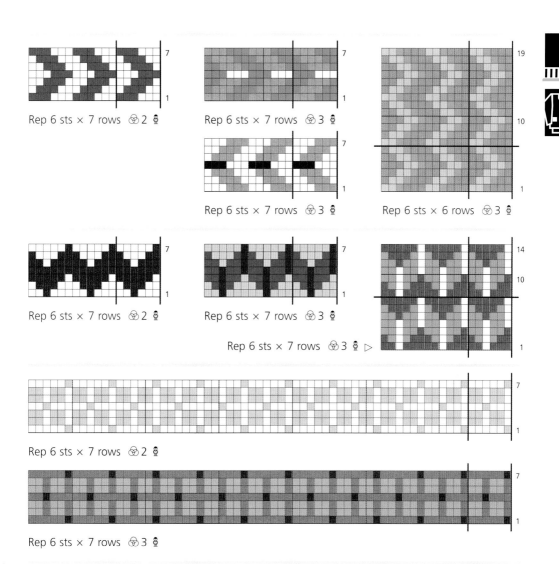

Rep 6 sts × 7 rows ⊛2 ☗

Rep 6 sts × 7 rows ⊛3 ☗

Rep 6 sts × 7 rows ⊛3 ☗

Rep 6 sts × 6 rows ⊛3 ☗

Rep 6 sts × 7 rows ⊛2 ☗

Rep 6 sts × 7 rows ⊛3 ☗

Rep 6 sts × 7 rows ⊛3 ☗ ▷

Rep 6 sts × 7 rows ⊛2 ☗

Rep 6 sts × 7 rows ⊛3 ☗

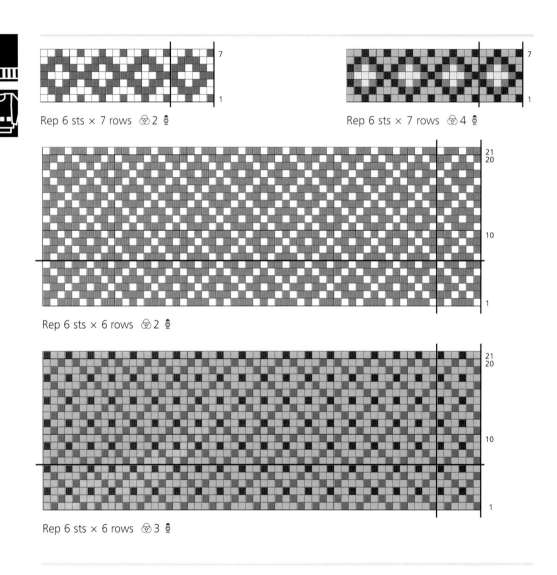

Rep 6 sts × 7 rows ⊛2 ⚀

Rep 6 sts × 7 rows ⊛4 ⚀

Rep 6 sts × 6 rows ⊛2 ⚀

Rep 6 sts × 6 rows ⊛3 ⚀

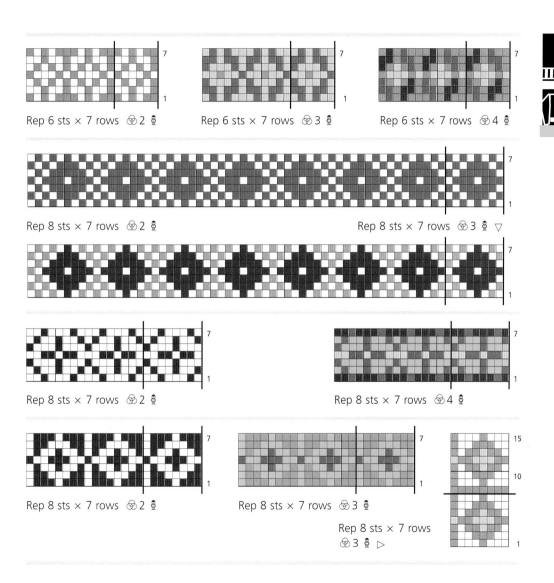

Rep 6 sts × 7 rows ⊛2 ⚱

Rep 6 sts × 7 rows ⊛3 ⚱

Rep 6 sts × 7 rows ⊛4 ⚱

Rep 8 sts × 7 rows ⊛2 ⚱

Rep 8 sts × 7 rows ⊛3 ⚱ ▽

Rep 8 sts × 7 rows ⊛2 ⚱

Rep 8 sts × 7 rows ⊛4 ⚱

Rep 8 sts × 7 rows ⊛2 ⚱

Rep 8 sts × 7 rows ⊛3 ⚱

Rep 8 sts × 7 rows ⊛3 ⚱ ▷

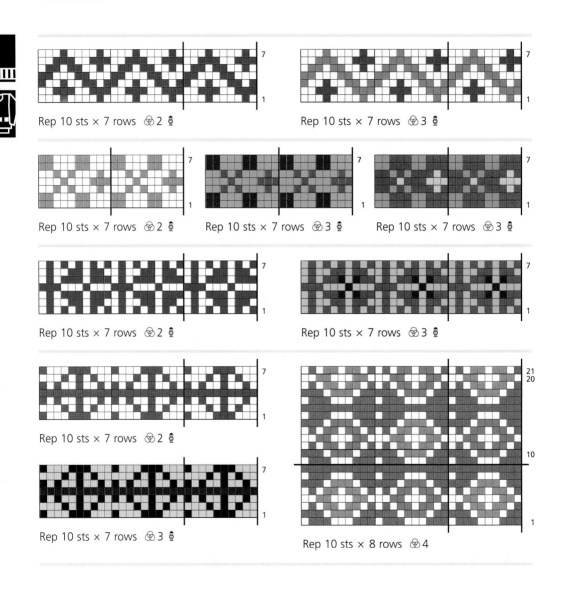

Rep 10 sts × 7 rows ⊛ 2 ⚲

Rep 10 sts × 7 rows ⊛ 3 ⚲

Rep 10 sts × 7 rows ⊛ 2 ⚲

Rep 10 sts × 7 rows ⊛ 3 ⚲

Rep 10 sts × 7 rows ⊛ 3 ⚲

Rep 10 sts × 7 rows ⊛ 2 ⚲

Rep 10 sts × 7 rows ⊛ 3 ⚲

Rep 10 sts × 7 rows ⊛ 2 ⚲

Rep 10 sts × 7 rows ⊛ 3 ⚲

Rep 10 sts × 8 rows ⊛ 4

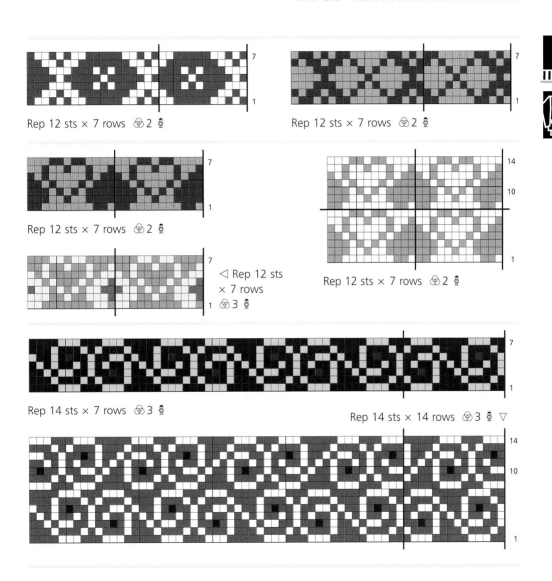

Rep 12 sts × 7 rows ⊛ 2 🕴

Rep 12 sts × 7 rows ⊛ 2 🕴

Rep 12 sts × 7 rows ⊛ 2 🕴

◁ Rep 12 sts
× 7 rows
⊛ 3 🕴

Rep 12 sts × 7 rows ⊛ 2 🕴

Rep 14 sts × 7 rows ⊛ 3 🕴

Rep 14 sts × 14 rows ⊛ 3 🕴 ▽

55

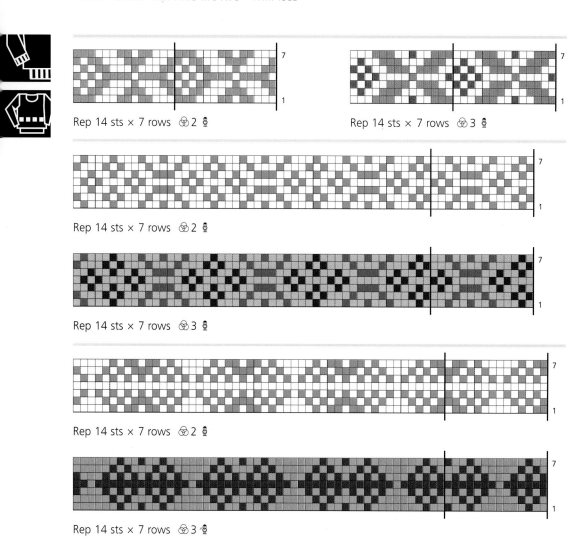

Rep 14 sts × 7 rows ⊛2 ☺

Rep 14 sts × 7 rows ⊛3 ☺

Rep 14 sts × 7 rows ⊛2 ☺

Rep 14 sts × 7 rows ⊛3 ☺

Rep 14 sts × 7 rows ⊛2 ☺

Rep 14 sts × 7 rows ⊛3 ☺

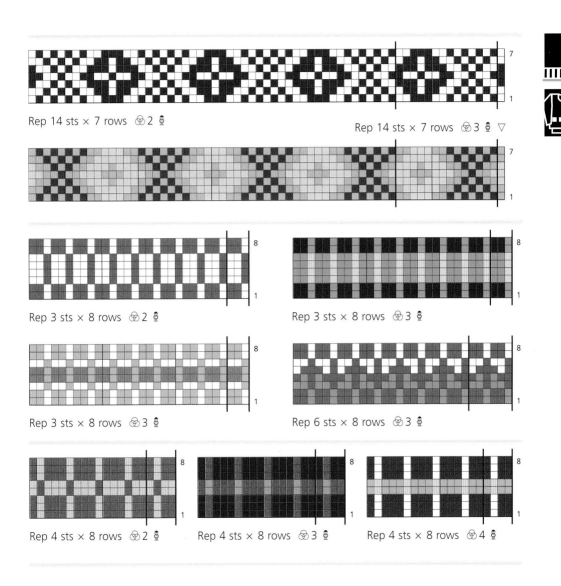

Rep 14 sts × 7 rows ⊛ 2 ⚇

Rep 14 sts × 7 rows ⊛ 3 ⚇ ▽

Rep 3 sts × 8 rows ⊛ 2 ⚇

Rep 3 sts × 8 rows ⊛ 3 ⚇

Rep 3 sts × 8 rows ⊛ 3 ⚇

Rep 6 sts × 8 rows ⊛ 3 ⚇

Rep 4 sts × 8 rows ⊛ 2 ⚇

Rep 4 sts × 8 rows ⊛ 3 ⚇

Rep 4 sts × 8 rows ⊛ 4 ⚇

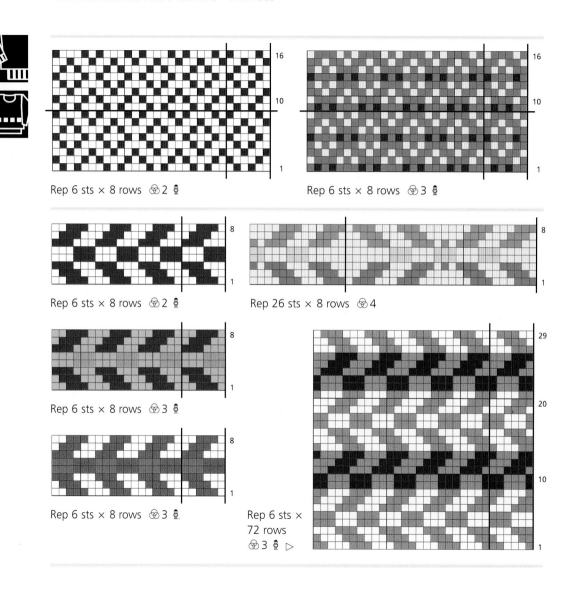

Rep 6 sts × 8 rows ⊛2 🦱

Rep 6 sts × 8 rows ⊛3 🦱

Rep 6 sts × 8 rows ⊛2 🦱

Rep 26 sts × 8 rows ⊛4

Rep 6 sts × 8 rows ⊛3 🦱

Rep 6 sts × 8 rows ⊛3 🦱

Rep 6 sts ×
72 rows
⊛3 🦱 ▷

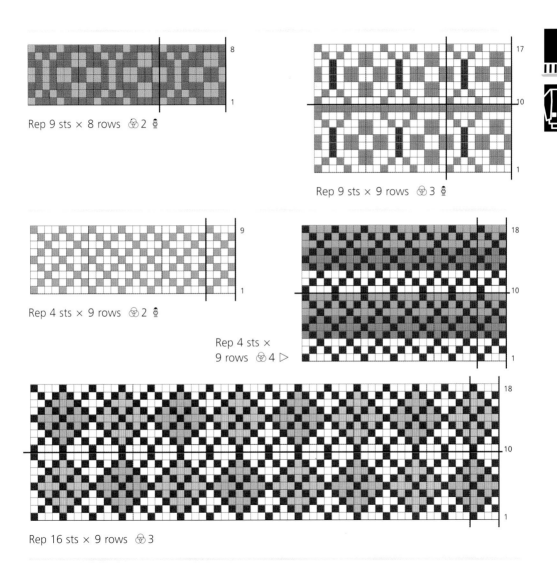

Rep 9 sts × 8 rows ⊛2 ⊛

Rep 9 sts × 9 rows ⊛3 ⊛

Rep 4 sts × 9 rows ⊛2 ⊛

Rep 4 sts ×
9 rows ⊛4 ▷

Rep 16 sts × 9 rows ⊛3

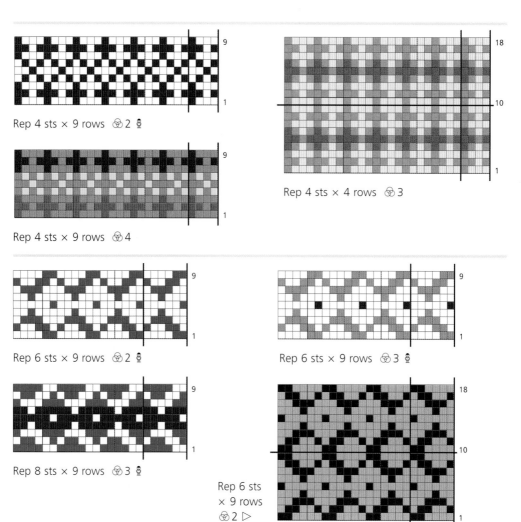

Rep 4 sts × 9 rows ⊛2 🔱

Rep 4 sts × 9 rows ⊛4

Rep 4 sts × 4 rows ⊛3

Rep 6 sts × 9 rows ⊛2 🔱

Rep 6 sts × 9 rows ⊛3 🔱

Rep 8 sts × 9 rows ⊛3 🔱

Rep 6 sts
× 9 rows
⊛2 ▷

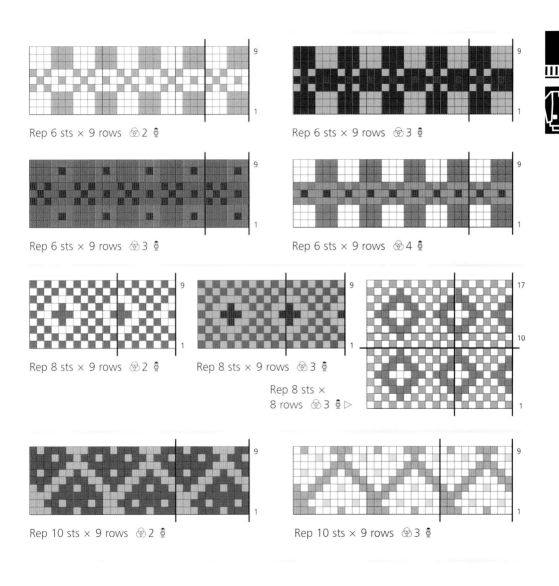

Rep 6 sts × 9 rows 🌐 2 🧍

Rep 6 sts × 9 rows 🌐 3 🧍

Rep 6 sts × 9 rows 🌐 3 🧍

Rep 6 sts × 9 rows 🌐 4 🧍

Rep 8 sts × 9 rows 🌐 2 🧍

Rep 8 sts × 9 rows 🌐 3 🧍

Rep 8 sts ×
8 rows 🌐 3 🧍 ▷

Rep 10 sts × 9 rows 🌐 2 🧍

Rep 10 sts × 9 rows 🌐 3 🧍

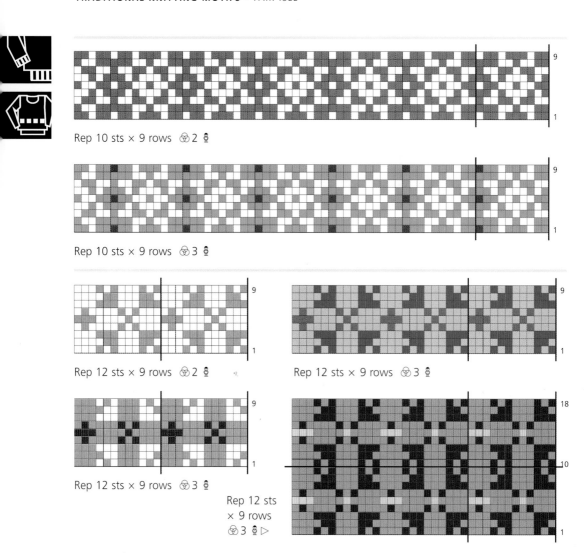

Rep 10 sts × 9 rows ⊛2 👤

Rep 10 sts × 9 rows ⊛3 👤

Rep 12 sts × 9 rows ⊛2 👤

Rep 12 sts × 9 rows ⊛3 👤

Rep 12 sts × 9 rows ⊛3 👤

Rep 12 sts
× 9 rows
⊛3 👤 ▷

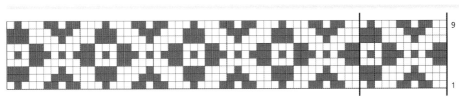

Rep 12 sts × 9 rows ⊛ 2 ♟

Rep 12 sts × 9 rows ⊛ 4

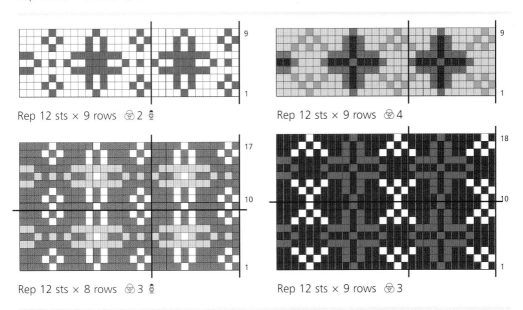

Rep 12 sts × 9 rows ⊛ 2 ♟

Rep 12 sts × 9 rows ⊛ 4

Rep 12 sts × 8 rows ⊛ 3 ♟

Rep 12 sts × 9 rows ⊛ 3

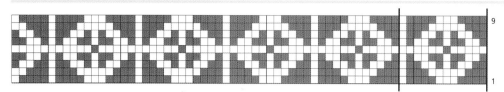

Rep 12 sts × 9 rows ⊛ 2 🎅

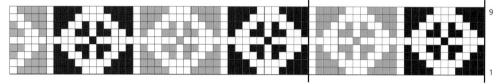

Rep 24 sts × 9 rows ⊛ 3 🎅

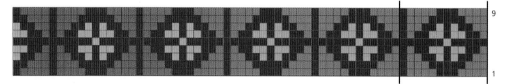

Rep 12 sts × 9 rows ⊛ 3 🎅

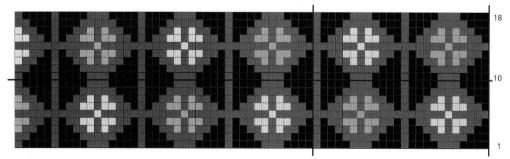

Rep 24 sts × 9 rows ⊛ 4

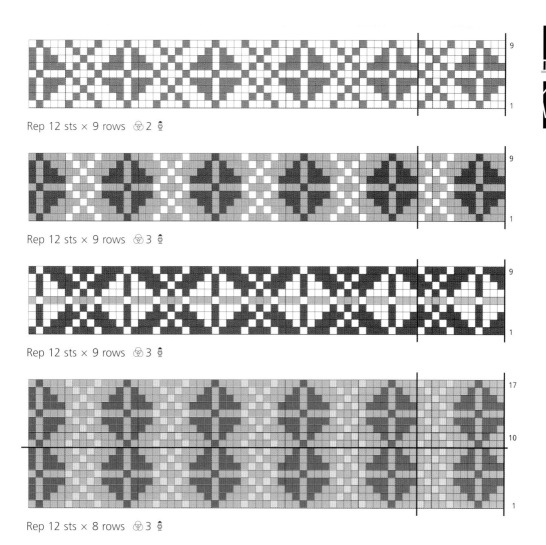

Rep 12 sts × 9 rows ⊛ 2 🧍

Rep 12 sts × 9 rows ⊛ 3 🧍

Rep 12 sts × 9 rows ⊛ 3 🧍

Rep 12 sts × 8 rows ⊛ 3 🧍

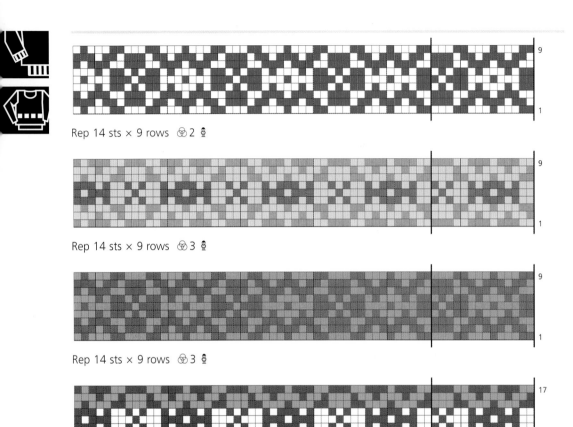

Rep 14 sts × 9 rows ⊛ 2 ⚇

Rep 14 sts × 9 rows ⊛ 3 ⚇

Rep 14 sts × 9 rows ⊛ 3 ⚇

Rep 14 sts × 8 rows ⊛ 3 ⚇

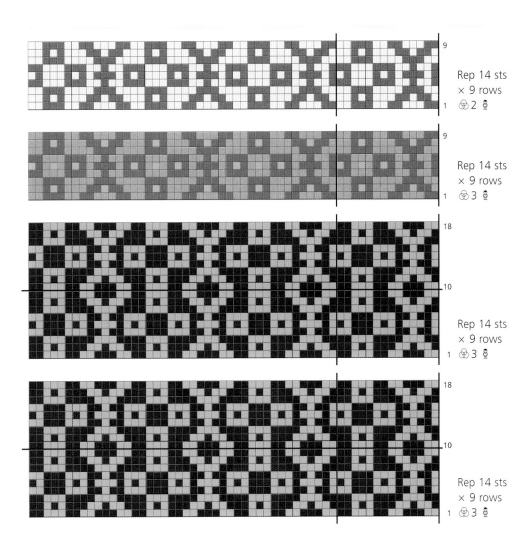

Rep 14 sts
× 9 rows
1 ⊛2 ♟

Rep 14 sts
× 9 rows
1 ⊛3 ♟

Rep 14 sts
× 9 rows
1 ⊛3 ♟

Rep 14 sts
× 9 rows
1 ⊛3 ♟

Rep 16 sts × 9 rows ⊗2 ⚇

Rep 16 sts × 9 rows ⊗5 ⚇

Rep 16 sts × 9 rows ⊗2 ⚇

Rep 16 sts × 18 rows ⊗4

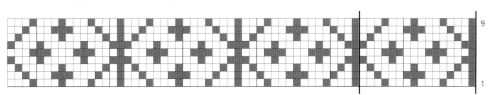

Rep 16 sts × 9 rows ⊛2 ⦵

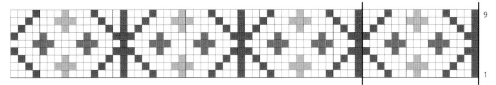

Rep 16 sts × 9 rows ⊛4

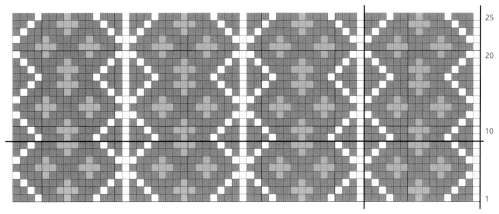

Rep 16 sts × 8 rows ⊛3

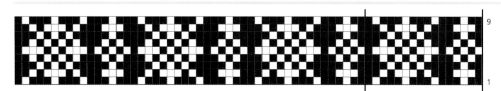

Rep 16 sts × 9 rows 🌀2 👤

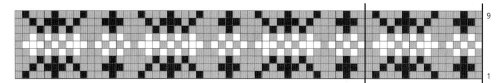

Rep 16 sts × 9 rows 🌀3 👤

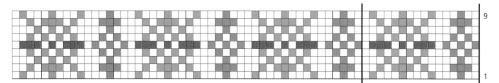

Rep 16 sts × 9 rows 🌀4

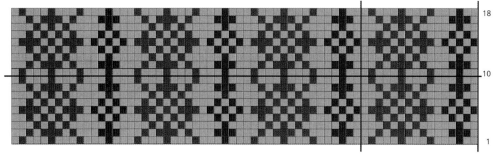

Rep 16 sts × 9 rows 🌀3

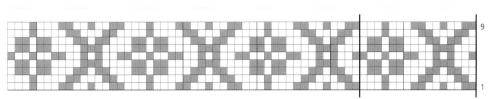

Rep 16 sts × 9 rows ⊛ 2 ⊛

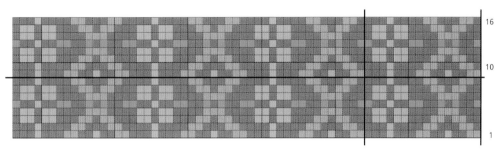

Rep 16 sts × 8 rows ⊛ 4

Rep 20 sts × 9 rows ⊛ 2 ⊛

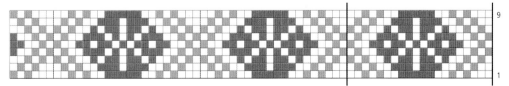

Rep 20 sts × 9 rows ⊛ 3

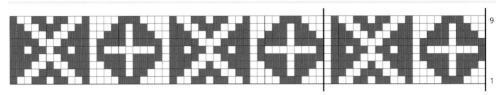

Rep 22 sts × 9 rows ⊛2 👤

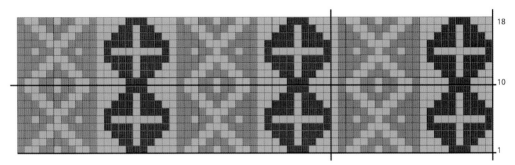

Rep 22 sts × 9 rows ⊛3 👤

Rep 22 sts × 9 rows ⊛2 👤 ▽

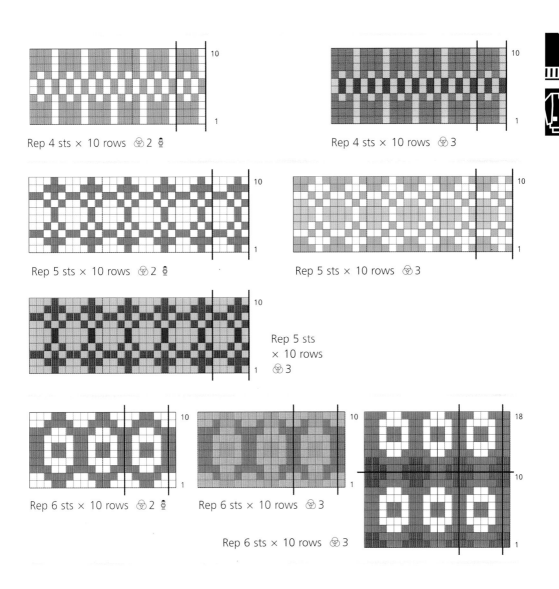

Rep 4 sts × 10 rows ⊛ 2 ⚇

Rep 4 sts × 10 rows ⊛ 3

Rep 5 sts × 10 rows ⊛ 2 ⚇

Rep 5 sts × 10 rows ⊛ 3

Rep 5 sts × 10 rows ⊛ 3

Rep 6 sts × 10 rows ⊛ 2 ⚇

Rep 6 sts × 10 rows ⊛ 3

Rep 6 sts × 10 rows ⊛ 3

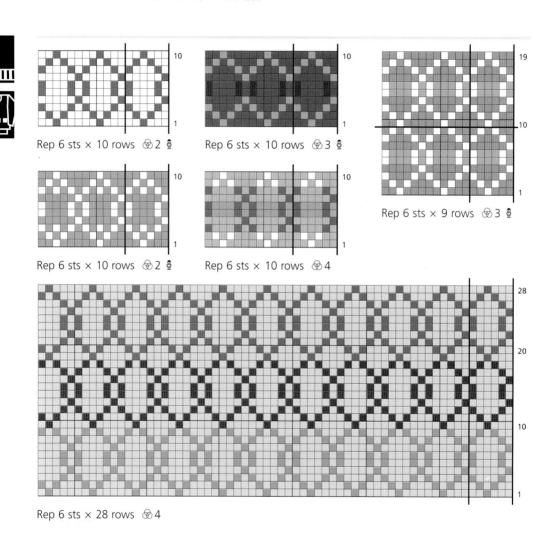

Rep 6 sts × 10 rows ⊛ 2 ₰

Rep 6 sts × 10 rows ⊛ 3 ₰

Rep 6 sts × 9 rows ⊛ 3 ₰

Rep 6 sts × 10 rows ⊛ 2 ₰

Rep 6 sts × 10 rows ⊛ 4

Rep 6 sts × 28 rows ⊛ 4

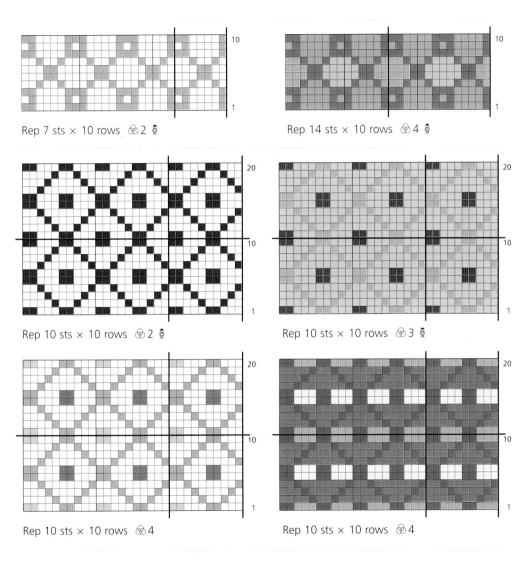

Rep 7 sts × 10 rows ⊛2 👤

Rep 14 sts × 10 rows ⊛4 👤

Rep 10 sts × 10 rows ⊛2 👤

Rep 10 sts × 10 rows ⊛3 👤

Rep 10 sts × 10 rows ⊛4

Rep 10 sts × 10 rows ⊛4

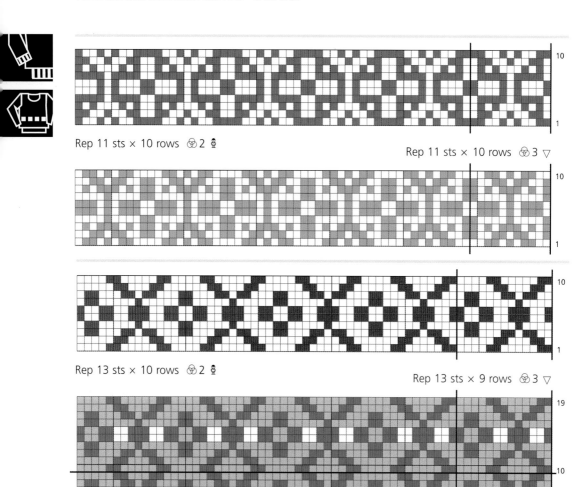

Rep 11 sts × 10 rows ⊛2 ⛄

Rep 11 sts × 10 rows ⊛3 ▽

Rep 13 sts × 10 rows ⊛2 ⛄

Rep 13 sts × 9 rows ⊛3 ▽

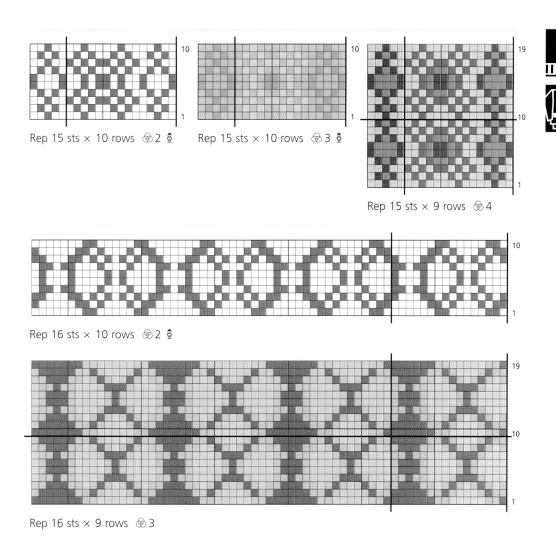

Rep 15 sts × 10 rows ⊛2 🎅

Rep 15 sts × 10 rows ⊛3 🎅

Rep 15 sts × 9 rows ⊛4

Rep 16 sts × 10 rows ⊛2 🎅

Rep 16 sts × 9 rows ⊛3

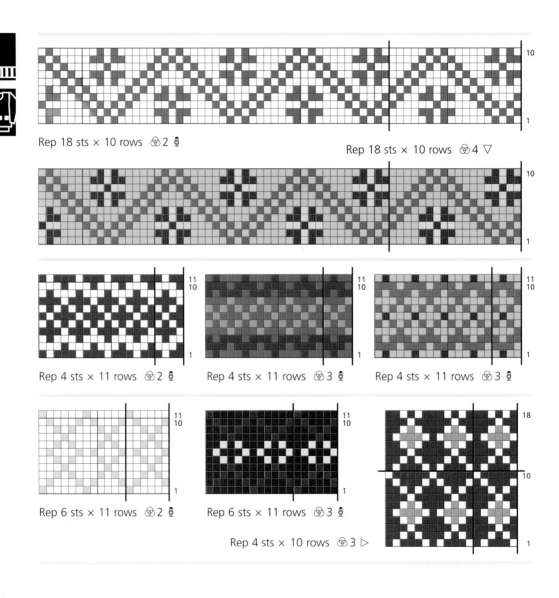

Rep 18 sts × 10 rows ⊛2 🯅

Rep 18 sts × 10 rows ⊛4 ▽

Rep 4 sts × 11 rows ⊛2 🯅

Rep 4 sts × 11 rows ⊛3 🯅

Rep 4 sts × 11 rows ⊛3 🯅

Rep 6 sts × 11 rows ⊛2 🯅

Rep 6 sts × 11 rows ⊛3 🯅

Rep 4 sts × 10 rows ⊛3 ▷

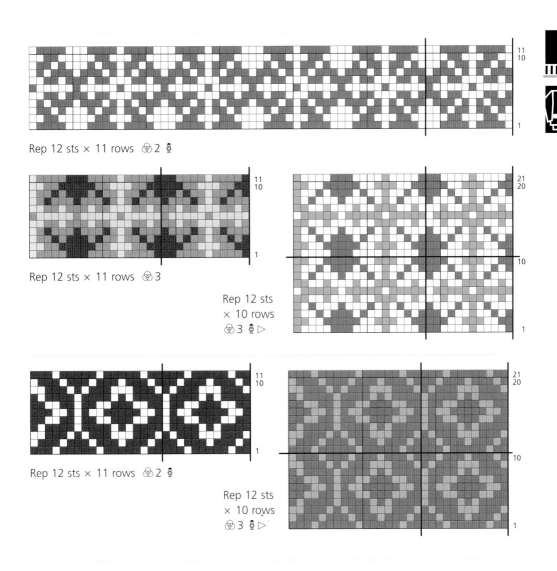

Rep 12 sts × 11 rows 🔆2 👤

Rep 12 sts × 11 rows 🔆3

Rep 12 sts
× 10 rows
🔆3 👤▷

Rep 12 sts × 11 rows 🔆2 👤

Rep 12 sts
× 10 rows
🔆3 👤▷

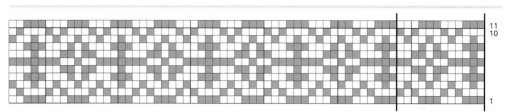

Rep 12 sts × 11 rows ⊛ 2 🯅

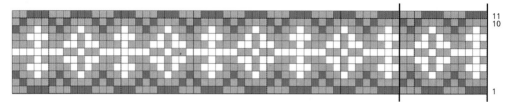

Rep 12 sts × 11 rows ⊛ 3

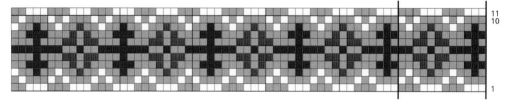

Rep 12 sts × 11 rows ⊛ 4

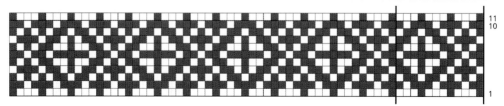

Rep 12 sts × 11 rows ⊛ 2 🯅. See page 81.

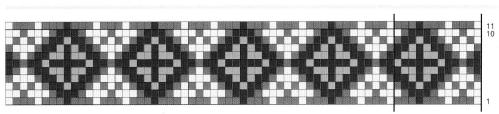

Rep 12 sts × 11 rows ⊛ 3. See page 80.

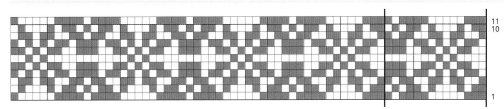

Rep 14 sts × 11 rows ⊛ 2 ⚇

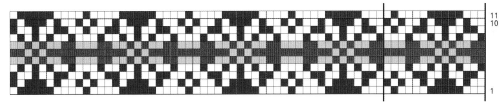

Rep 14 sts × 11 rows ⊛ 4

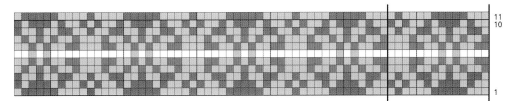

Rep 14 sts × 11 rows ⊛ 4

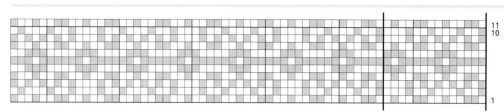

Rep 14 sts × 11 rows ⊗ 2 ▮

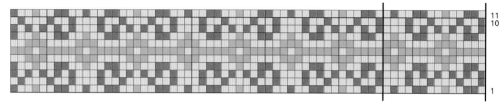

Rep 14 sts × 11 rows ⊗ 3 ▮

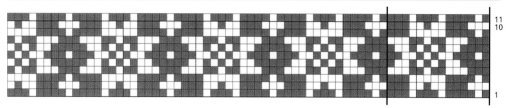

Rep 14 sts × 11 rows ⊗ 2 ▮

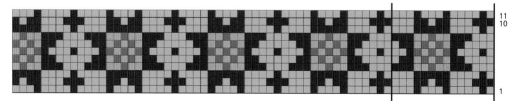

Rep 14 sts × 11 rows ⊗ 4

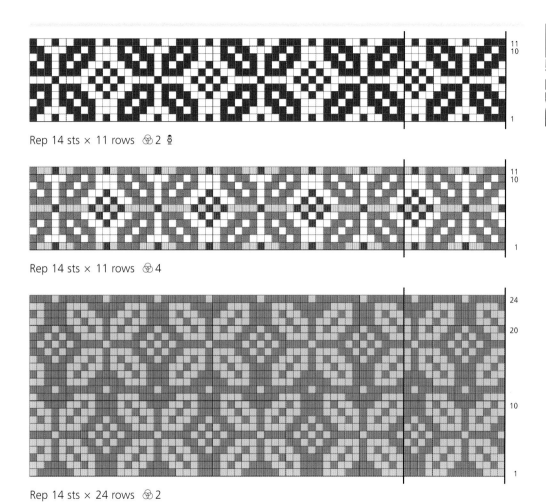

Rep 14 sts × 11 rows ⊛2 ⎸

Rep 14 sts × 11 rows ⊛4

Rep 14 sts × 24 rows ⊛2

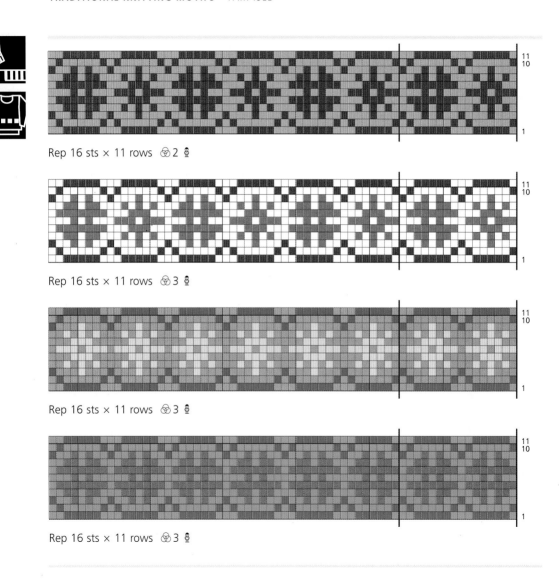

Rep 16 sts × 11 rows ⊛2 ⚇

Rep 16 sts × 11 rows ⊛3 ⚇

Rep 16 sts × 11 rows ⊛3 ⚇

Rep 16 sts × 11 rows ⊛3 ⚇

Rep 20 sts × 11 rows ⊗ 2 ⚇

Rep 20 sts × 11 rows ⊗ 4

Rep 26 sts × 11 rows ⊗ 2

Rep 26 sts × 11 rows ⊗ 3

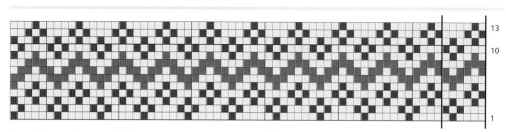

Rep 6 sts × 13 rows ✲3

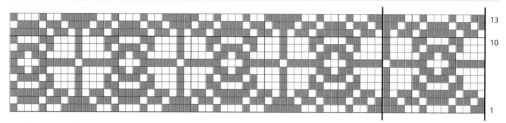

Rep 14 sts × 13 rows ✲2 ⚇

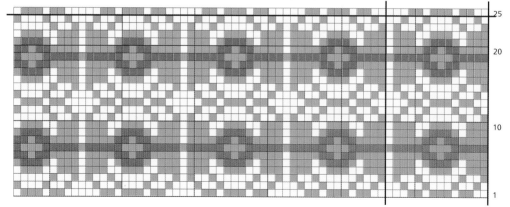

Rep 14 sts × 24 rows ✲4

Rep 16 sts × 14 rows ⊛ 3

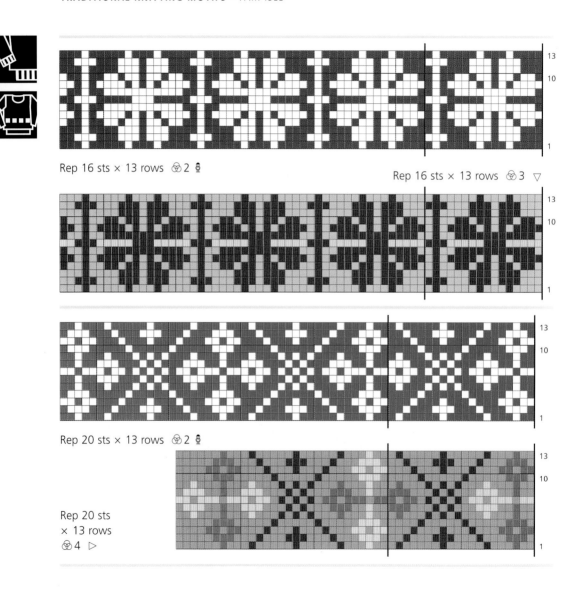

Rep 16 sts × 13 rows ⊛2 ⚲

Rep 16 sts × 13 rows ⊛3 ▽

Rep 20 sts × 13 rows ⊛2 ⚲

Rep 20 sts
× 13 rows
⊛4 ▷

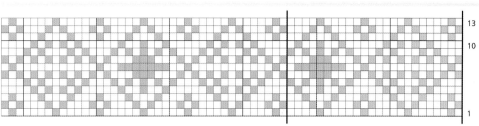

Rep 24 sts × 13 rows ⊛ 2 ⚇

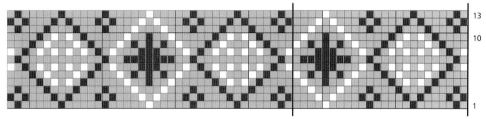

Rep 24 sts × 13 rows ⊛ 3

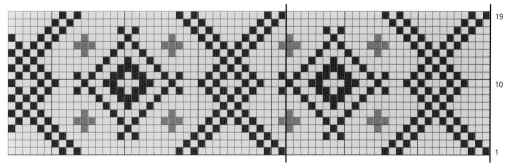

Rep 28 sts × 19 rows ⊛ 3

89

Scandinavia

Norway, Finland, Sweden and Denmark have a long knitting tradition and share many motifs with the Shetland Islands, as seen in the previous chapter. However, their style of knitting and approach to motifs are slightly different. Norwegian knitting favors small geometric motifs; the simple cross, the diamond and the swastika in light and dark yarns or often just black and white. The same simple shapes are found in traditional Finnish knitting but the same two color motifs are in vibrant colors which change every few rows. Both Swedish and Danish traditional knitting is influenced by the folk images of Northern Europe; naive images of nature, landscape and folk dress in bright colors.

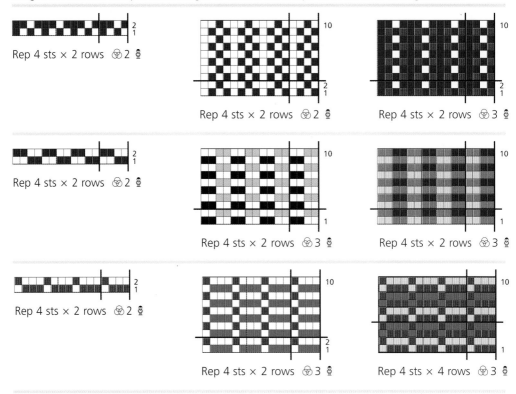

Rep 4 sts × 2 rows ⊛2 🕯

Rep 4 sts × 2 rows ⊛2 🕯

Rep 4 sts × 2 rows ⊛3 🕯

Rep 4 sts × 2 rows ⊛2 🕯

Rep 4 sts × 2 rows ⊛3 🕯

Rep 4 sts × 2 rows ⊛3 🕯

Rep 4 sts × 2 rows ⊛2 🕯

Rep 4 sts × 2 rows ⊛3 🕯

Rep 4 sts × 4 rows ⊛3 🕯

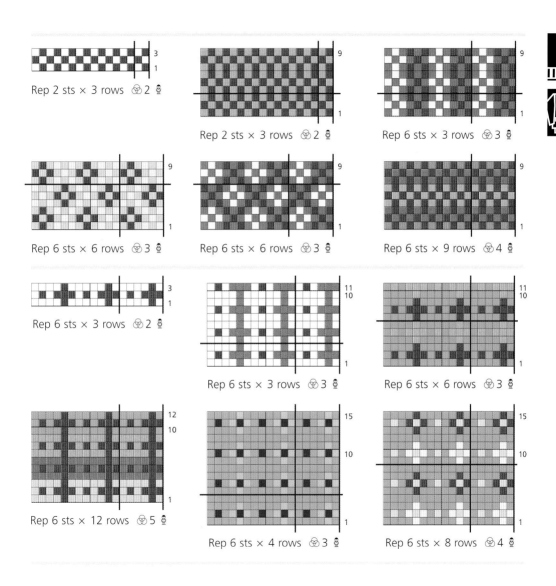

Rep 2 sts × 3 rows ⊛ 2 ♟

Rep 2 sts × 3 rows ⊛ 2 ♟

Rep 6 sts × 3 rows ⊛ 3 ♟

Rep 6 sts × 6 rows ⊛ 3 ♟

Rep 6 sts × 6 rows ⊛ 3 ♟

Rep 6 sts × 9 rows ⊛ 4 ♟

Rep 6 sts × 3 rows ⊛ 2 ♟

Rep 6 sts × 3 rows ⊛ 3 ♟

Rep 6 sts × 6 rows ⊛ 3 ♟

Rep 6 sts × 12 rows ⊛ 5 ♟

Rep 6 sts × 4 rows ⊛ 3 ♟

Rep 6 sts × 8 rows ⊛ 4 ♟

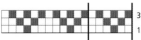

Rep 6 sts × 3 rows ⊛2 ⛄

Rep 6 sts × 5 rows ⊛4 ⛄

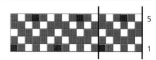

Rep 6 sts × 5 rows ⊛3 ⛄

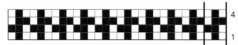

Rep 3 sts × 4 rows ⊛2 ⛄

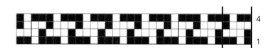

Rep 4 sts × 4 rows ⊛2 ⛄

Rep 4 sts × 5 rows ⊛2 ⛄

Rep 4 sts × 4 rows
⊛2 ⛄

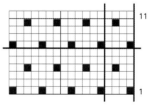

Rep 4 sts × 6 rows
⊛2 ⛄

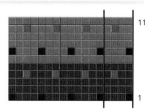

Rep 4 sts × 11 rows
⊛4

Rep 4 sts × 4 rows
⊛2 ⛄

Rep 4 sts × 4 rows
⊛2 ⛄

Rep 4 sts × 7 rows ⊛3 ⛄

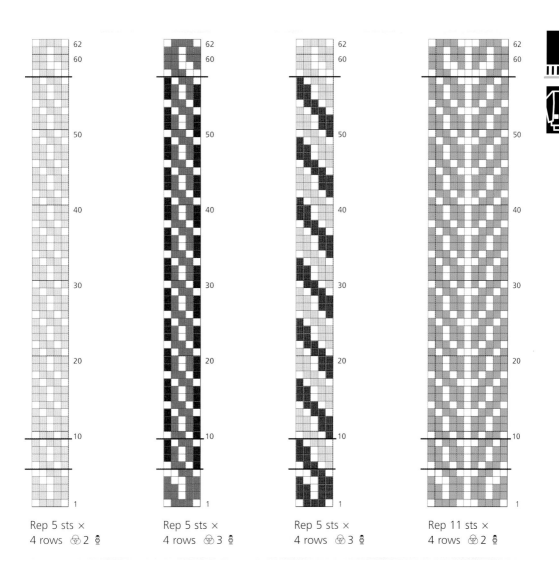

Rep 5 sts ×
4 rows ⊛2 ⚇

Rep 5 sts ×
4 rows ⊛3 ⚇

Rep 5 sts ×
4 rows ⊛3 ⚇

Rep 11 sts ×
4 rows ⊛2 ⚇

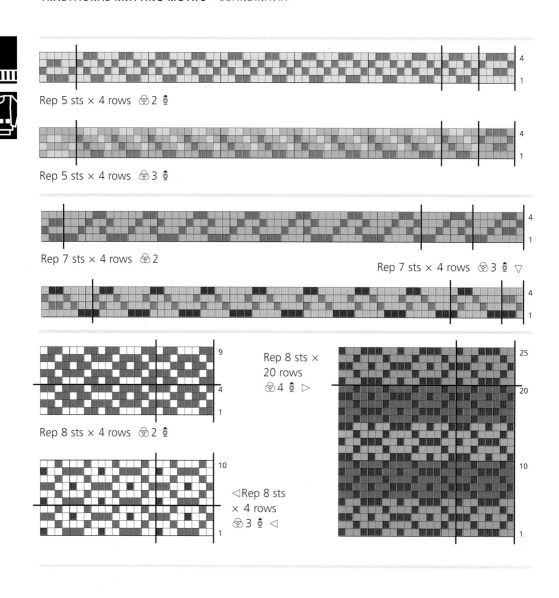

Rep 5 sts × 4 rows ⊛ 2 ♟

Rep 5 sts × 4 rows ⊛ 3 ♟

Rep 7 sts × 4 rows ⊛ 2

Rep 7 sts × 4 rows ⊛ 3 ♟ ▽

Rep 8 sts × 4 rows ⊛ 2 ♟

Rep 8 sts ×
20 rows
⊛ 4 ♟ ▷

◁ Rep 8 sts
× 4 rows
⊛ 3 ♟ ◁

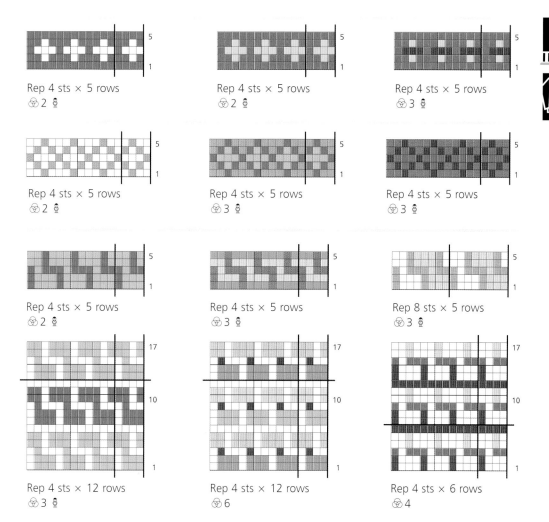

Rep 4 sts × 5 rows
2

Rep 4 sts × 5 rows
2

Rep 4 sts × 5 rows
3

Rep 4 sts × 5 rows
2

Rep 4 sts × 5 rows
3

Rep 4 sts × 5 rows
3

Rep 4 sts × 5 rows
2

Rep 4 sts × 5 rows
3

Rep 8 sts × 5 rows
3

Rep 4 sts × 12 rows
3

Rep 4 sts × 12 rows
6

Rep 4 sts × 6 rows
4

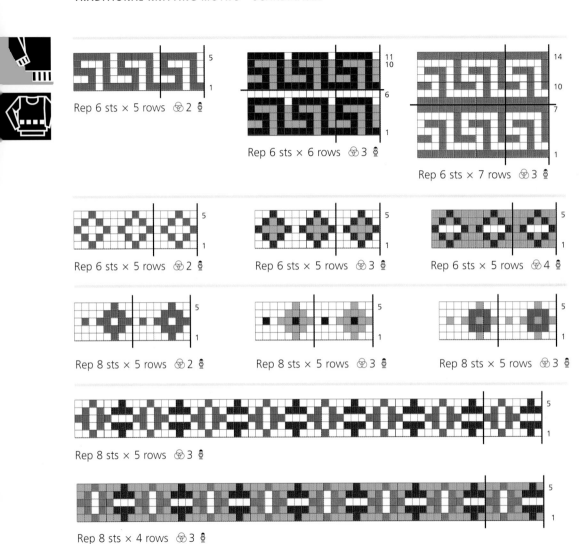

Rep 6 sts × 5 rows ✿ 2 🯅

Rep 6 sts × 6 rows ✿ 3 🯅

Rep 6 sts × 7 rows ✿ 3 🯅

Rep 6 sts × 5 rows ✿ 2 🯅

Rep 6 sts × 5 rows ✿ 3 🯅

Rep 6 sts × 5 rows ✿ 4 🯅

Rep 8 sts × 5 rows ✿ 2 🯅

Rep 8 sts × 5 rows ✿ 3 🯅

Rep 8 sts × 5 rows ✿ 3 🯅

Rep 8 sts × 5 rows ✿ 3 🯅

Rep 8 sts × 4 rows ✿ 3 🯅

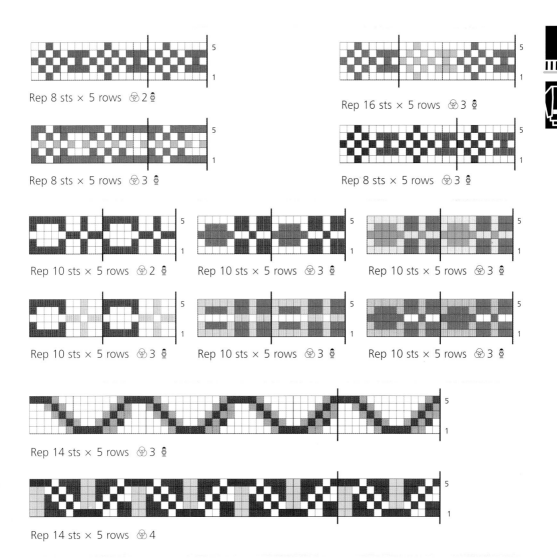

Rep 8 sts × 5 rows ⊛ 2 ♟

Rep 16 sts × 5 rows ⊛ 3 ♟

Rep 8 sts × 5 rows ⊛ 3 ♟

Rep 8 sts × 5 rows ⊛ 3 ♟

Rep 10 sts × 5 rows ⊛ 2 ♟

Rep 10 sts × 5 rows ⊛ 3 ♟

Rep 10 sts × 5 rows ⊛ 3 ♟

Rep 10 sts × 5 rows ⊛ 3 ♟

Rep 10 sts × 5 rows ⊛ 3 ♟

Rep 10 sts × 5 rows ⊛ 3 ♟

Rep 14 sts × 5 rows ⊛ 3 ♟

Rep 14 sts × 5 rows ⊛ 4

Rep 14 sts × 5 rows
⊗ 2

Rep 14 sts × 15 rows
⊗ 4

Rep 14 sts × 5 rows ⊗ 3

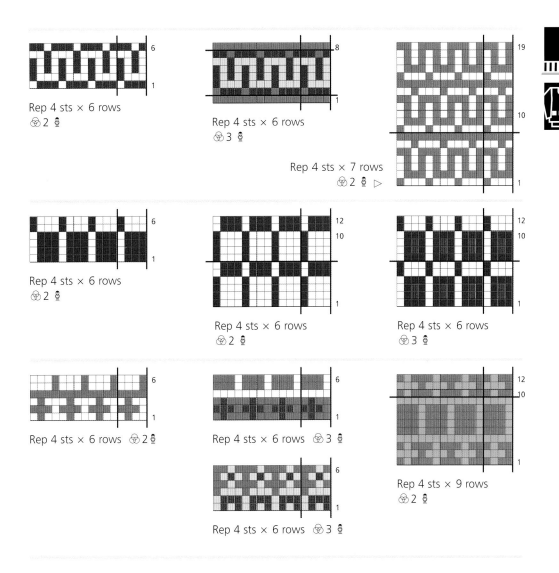

Rep 4 sts × 6 rows
🔘 2 👤

Rep 4 sts × 6 rows
🔘 3 👤

Rep 4 sts × 7 rows
🔘 2 👤 ▷

Rep 4 sts × 6 rows
🔘 2 👤

Rep 4 sts × 6 rows
🔘 2 👤

Rep 4 sts × 6 rows
🔘 3 👤

Rep 4 sts × 6 rows 🔘 2 👤

Rep 4 sts × 6 rows 🔘 3 👤

Rep 4 sts × 9 rows
🔘 2 👤

Rep 4 sts × 6 rows 🔘 3 👤

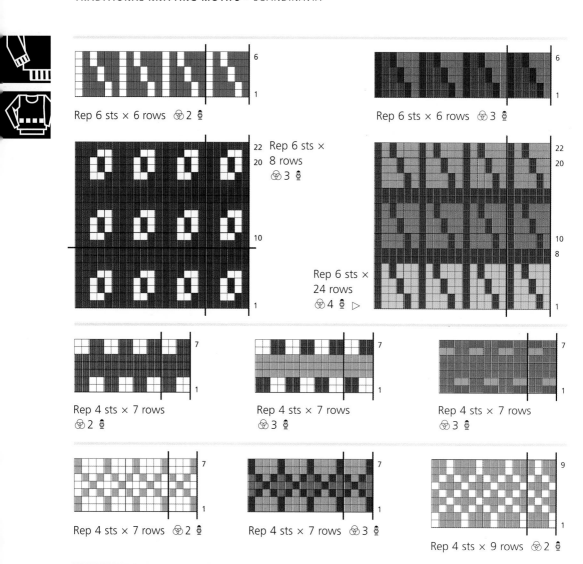

Rep 6 sts × 6 rows ⊛2 ⚱

Rep 6 sts × 6 rows ⊛3 ⚱

Rep 6 sts × 8 rows ⊛3 ⚱

Rep 6 sts × 24 rows ⊛4 ⚱ ▷

Rep 4 sts × 7 rows ⊛2 ⚱

Rep 4 sts × 7 rows ⊛3 ⚱

Rep 4 sts × 7 rows ⊛3 ⚱

Rep 4 sts × 7 rows ⊛2 ⚱

Rep 4 sts × 7 rows ⊛3 ⚱

Rep 4 sts × 9 rows ⊛2 ⚱

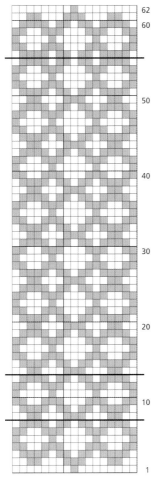

Rep 17 sts × 6 rows ⊛ 2

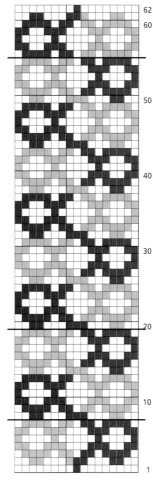

Rep 17 sts × 12 rows ⊛ 3

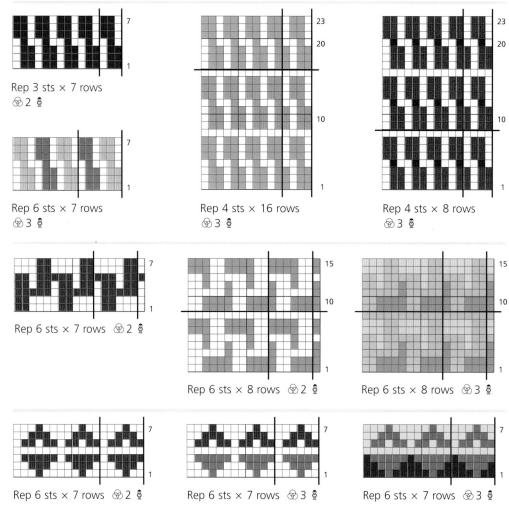

Rep 3 sts × 7 rows
⊛2 ☗

Rep 6 sts × 7 rows
⊛3 ☗

Rep 4 sts × 16 rows
⊛3 ☗

Rep 4 sts × 8 rows
⊛3 ☗

Rep 6 sts × 7 rows ⊛2 ☗

Rep 6 sts × 8 rows ⊛2 ☗

Rep 6 sts × 8 rows ⊛3 ☗

Rep 6 sts × 7 rows ⊛2 ☗

Rep 6 sts × 7 rows ⊛3 ☗

Rep 6 sts × 7 rows ⊛3 ☗

Rep 6 sts × 7 rows 3

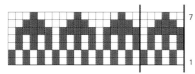

Rep 6 sts × 7 rows 2

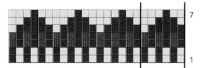

Rep 6 sts × 7 rows 3

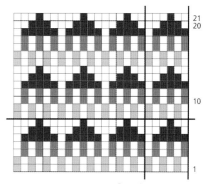

Rep 6 sts × 7 rows 4

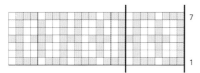

Rep 8 sts × 7 rows 2

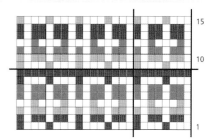

Rep 8 sts × 8 rows 4

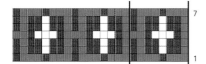

Rep 8 sts × 7 rows 3

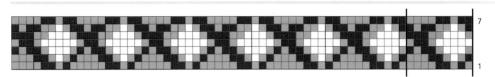

Rep 9 sts × 7 rows ⊛3 ⓯

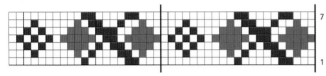

Rep 21 sts × 7 rows
⊛ 3

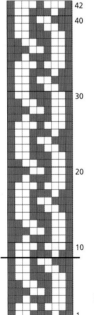

Rep 9 sts × 8 rows
⊛ 2 ⓯

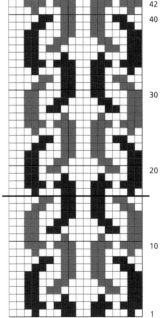

Rep 9 sts × 16 rows
⊛ 3

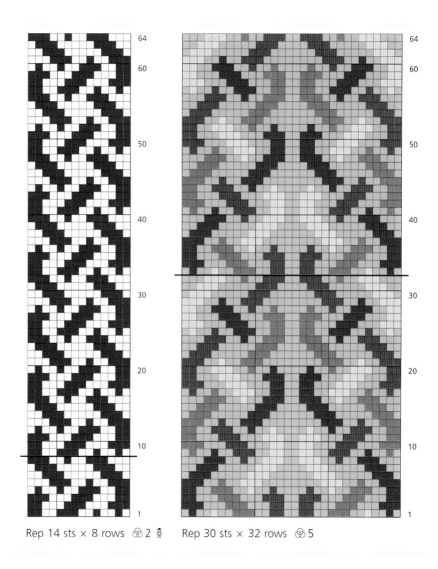

Rep 14 sts × 8 rows ⊛2 🧵   Rep 30 sts × 32 rows ⊛5

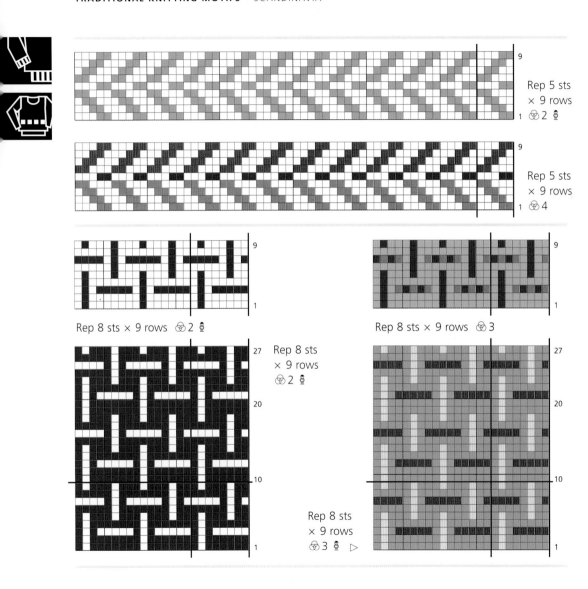

Rep 5 sts
× 9 rows
⊛2 🯅

Rep 5 sts
× 9 rows
⊛4

Rep 8 sts × 9 rows ⊛2 🯅

Rep 8 sts × 9 rows ⊛3

Rep 8 sts
× 9 rows
⊛2 🯅

Rep 8 sts
× 9 rows
⊛3 🯅 ▷

Rep 12 sts × 9 rows ⊛ 2 ⬮

Rep 12 sts × 9 rows ⊛ 3

Rep 12 sts × 9 rows ⊛ 2 ⬮

Rep 12 sts × 9 rows ⊛ 2 ⬮

Rep 12 sts × 11 rows ⊛ 2 ⬮

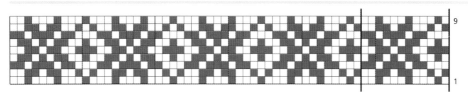

Rep 12 sts × 9 rows ⊛ 2 ⚇

Rep 12 sts × 9 rows ⊛ 3

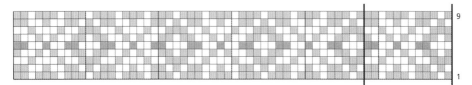

Rep 12 sts × 9 rows ⊛ 3

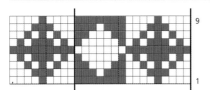

Rep 16 sts × 9 rows ⊛ 2 ⚇

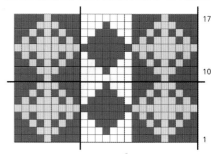

Rep 16 sts × 8 rows ⊛ 3

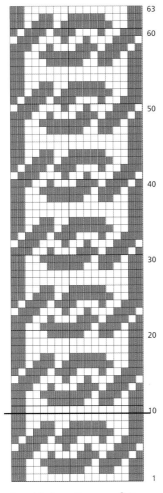

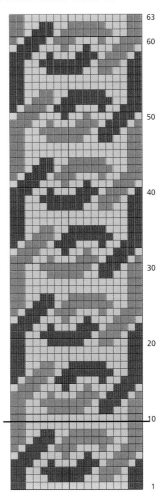

Rep 18 sts × 9 rows ⊛ 2

Rep 18 sts × 9 rows ⊛ 3

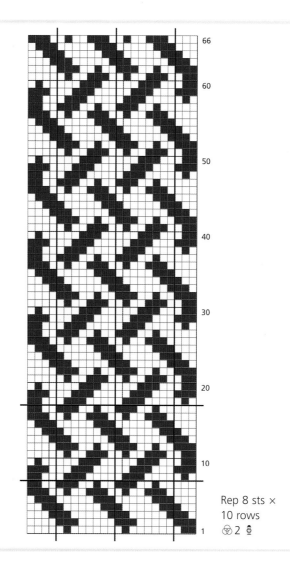

Rep 8 sts ×
10 rows
⊛ 2 🜍

Rep 8 sts ×
10 rows
⊛2 🯅

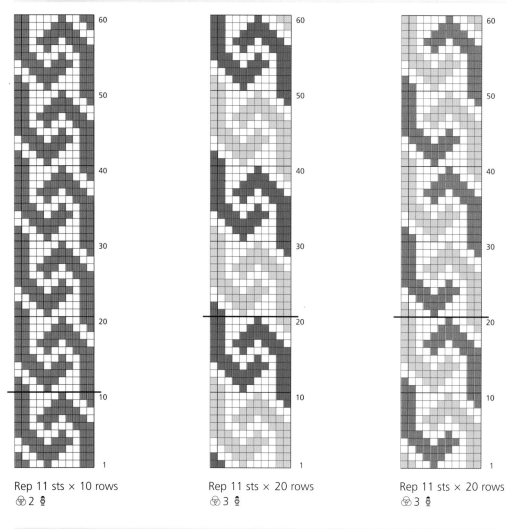

Rep 11 sts × 10 rows
⊛2 🎅

Rep 11 sts × 20 rows
⊛3 🎅

Rep 11 sts × 20 rows
⊛3 🎅

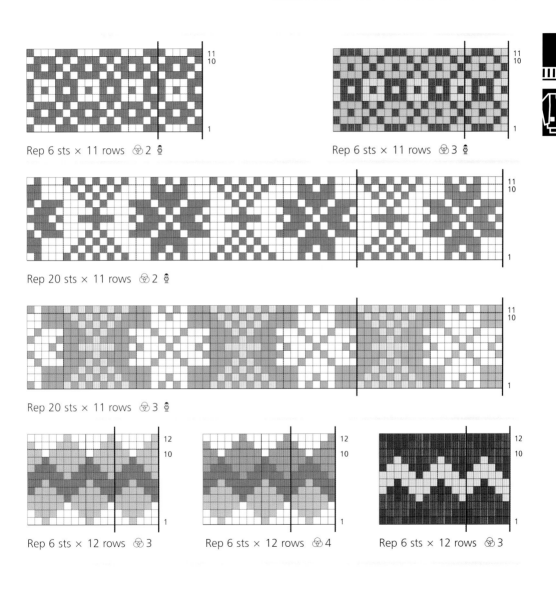

Rep 6 sts × 11 rows ⊛2 ⚇

Rep 6 sts × 11 rows ⊛3 ⚇

Rep 20 sts × 11 rows ⊛2 ⚇

Rep 20 sts × 11 rows ⊛3 ⚇

Rep 6 sts × 12 rows ⊛3

Rep 6 sts × 12 rows ⊛4

Rep 6 sts × 12 rows ⊛3

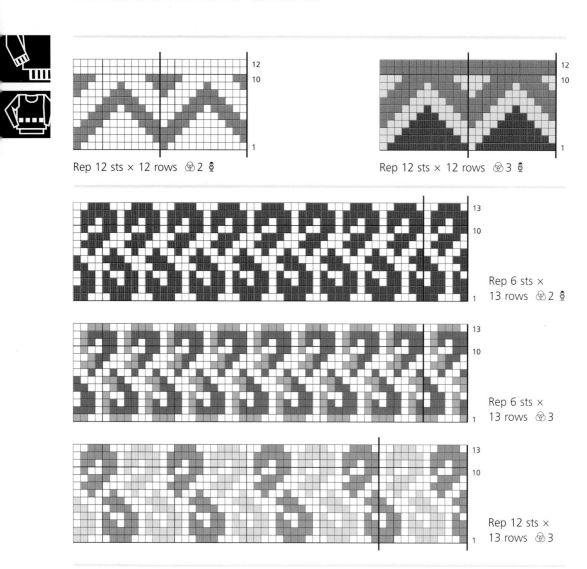

Rep 12 sts × 12 rows ⊛2 ⛶

Rep 12 sts × 12 rows ⊛3 ⛶

Rep 6 sts × 13 rows ⊛2 ⛶

Rep 6 sts × 13 rows ⊛3

Rep 12 sts × 13 rows ⊛3

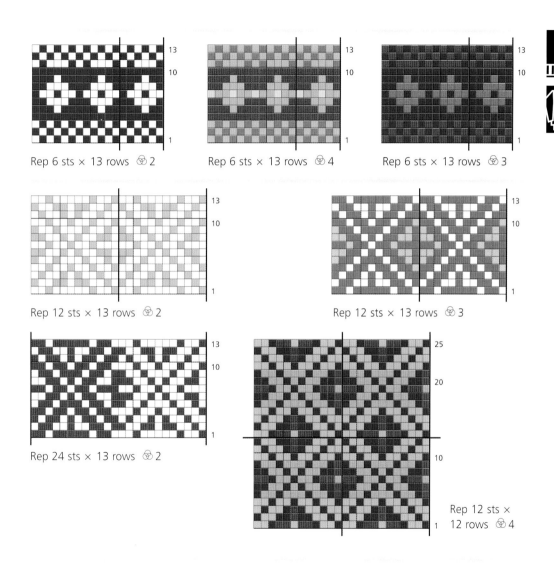

Rep 6 sts × 13 rows ✾ 2

Rep 6 sts × 13 rows ✾ 4

Rep 6 sts × 13 rows ✾ 3

Rep 12 sts × 13 rows ✾ 2

Rep 12 sts × 13 rows ✾ 3

Rep 24 sts × 13 rows ✾ 2

Rep 12 sts ×
12 rows ✾ 4

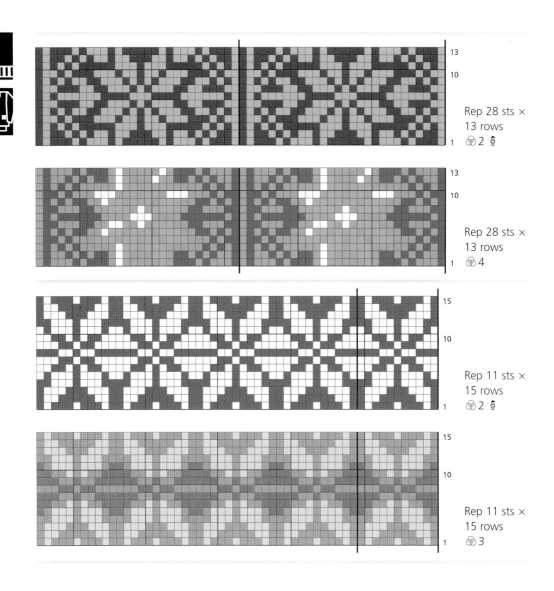

Rep 28 sts ×
13 rows
⊛2 ⚇

Rep 28 sts ×
13 rows
⊛4

Rep 11 sts ×
15 rows
⊛2 ⚇

Rep 11 sts ×
15 rows
⊛3

Rep 11 sts ×
14 rows ✿2
See page 116.

Rep 16 sts ×
15 rows ✿2

Rep 16 sts ×
15 rows ✿3

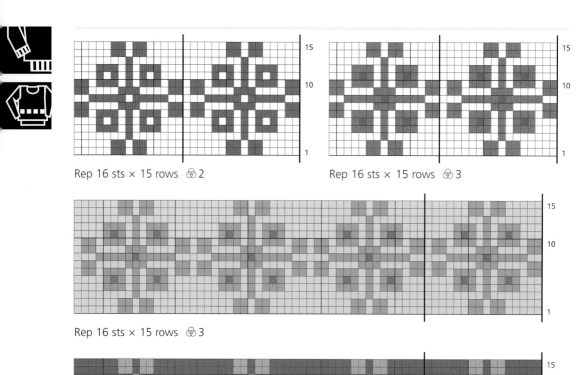

Rep 16 sts × 15 rows ⊛ 2

Rep 16 sts × 15 rows ⊛ 3

Rep 16 sts × 15 rows ⊛ 3

Rep 16 sts × 15 rows ⊛ 4

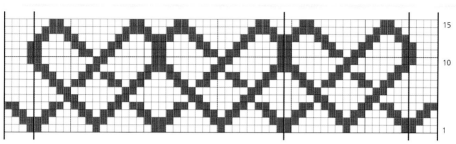

Rep 17 sts × 15 rows ⊛ 2 ⌂

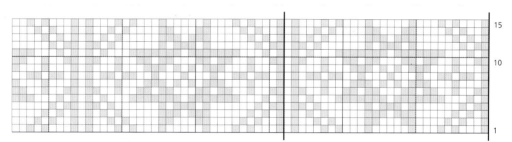

Rep 28 sts × 15 rows ⊛ 2

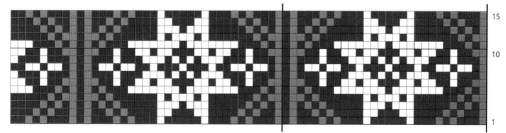

Rep 28 sts × 15 rows ⊛ 3

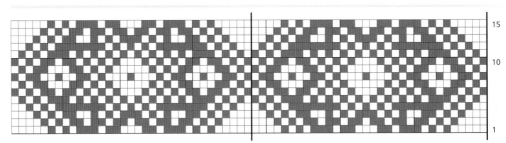

Rep 32 sts × 15 rows ⊛ 2

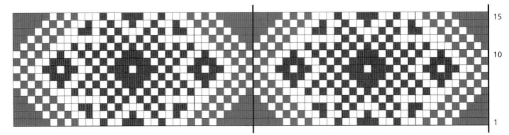

Rep 32 sts × 15 rows ⊛ 3

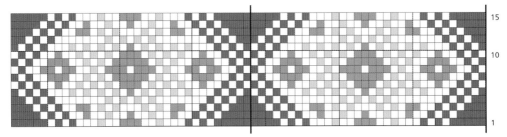

Rep 32 sts × 15 rows ⊛ 4

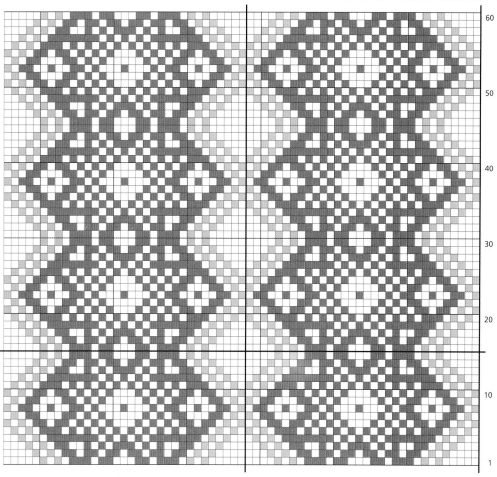

Rep 32 sts × 15 rows ⊛ 3

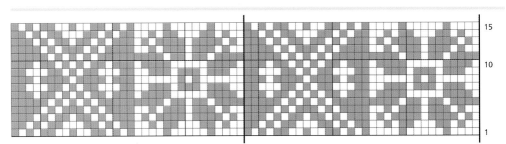

Rep 32 sts × 15 rows ⊛ 2

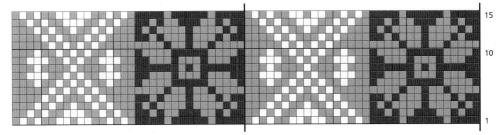

Rep 32 sts × 15 rows ⊛ 3

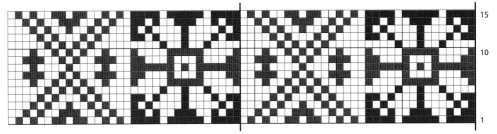

Rep 32 sts × 15 rows ⊛ 3

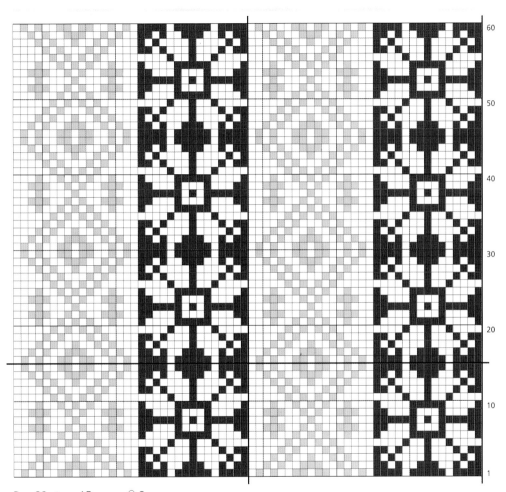

Rep 32 sts × 15 rows ⊛ 3

Rep 12 sts × 17 rows ⊛2 🧶

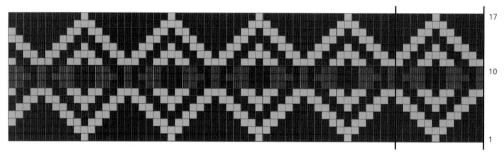

Rep 12 sts × 17 rows ⊛3

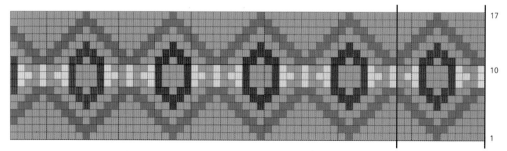

Rep 12 sts × 17 rows ⊛4

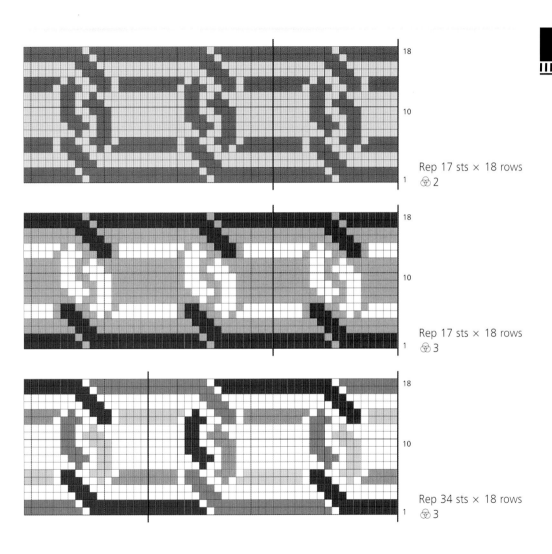

Rep 17 sts × 18 rows
⊛ 2

Rep 17 sts × 18 rows
⊛ 3

Rep 34 sts × 18 rows
⊛ 3

Rep 12 sts × 19 rows ⊛ 2

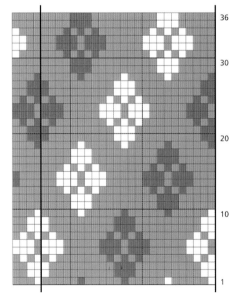

Rep 24 sts × 36 rows ⊛ 3

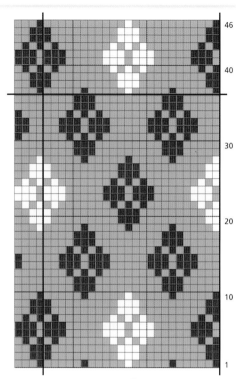

Rep 24 sts × 36 rows ⊛ 3

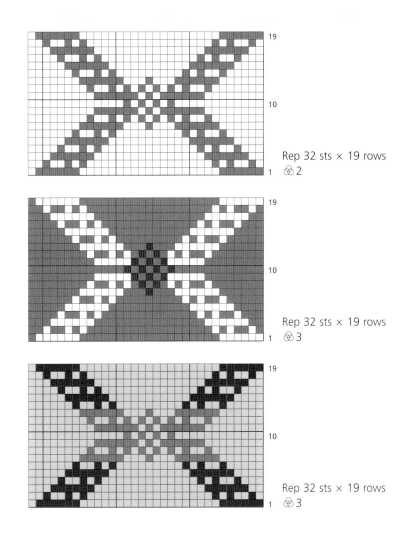

Rep 32 sts × 19 rows
⊛ 2

Rep 32 sts × 19 rows
⊛ 3

Rep 32 sts × 19 rows
⊛ 3

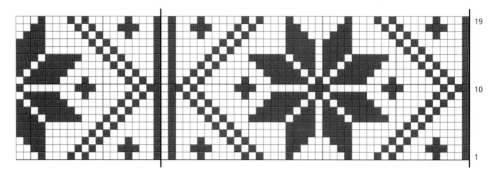

Rep 42 sts × 19 rows ⊛ 2

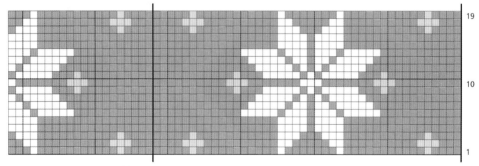

Rep 42 sts × 19 rows ⊛ 4

Rep 24 sts × 24 rows ⊛ 3

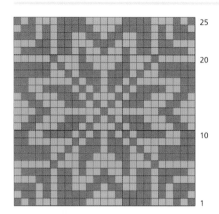

Rep 25 sts × 25 rows ⊛ 2

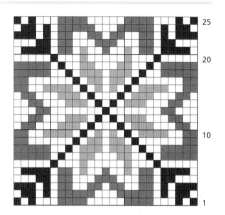

Rep 25 sts × 25 rows ⊛ 4

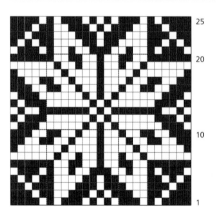

Rep 25 sts × 25 rows ⊛ 2

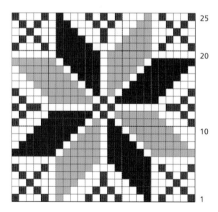

Rep 25 sts × 25 rows ⊛ 4

Rep 24 sts × 24 rows ⊛ 2

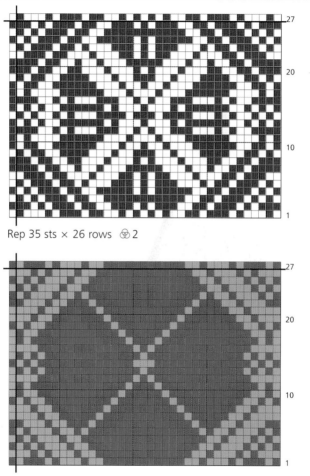

Rep 35 sts × 26 rows ⊛ 2

Rep 35 sts × 26 rows ⊛ 3

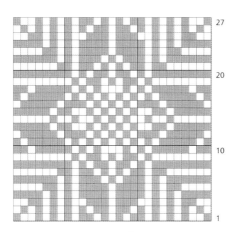

Rep 27 sts × 27 rows ⊛ 2

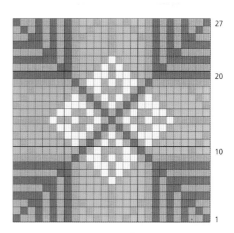

Rep 27 sts × 27 rows ⊛ 4

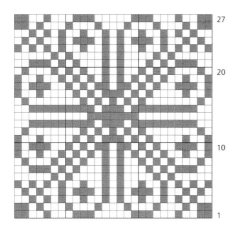

Rep 27 sts × 27 rows ⊛ 2

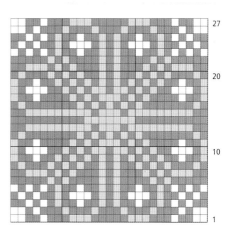

Rep 27 sts × 27 rows ⊛ 3

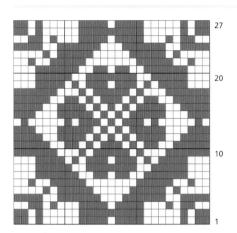

Rep 27 sts × 27 rows ⊛ 2

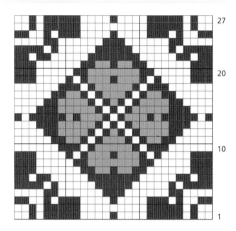

Rep 27 sts × 27 rows ⊛ 3

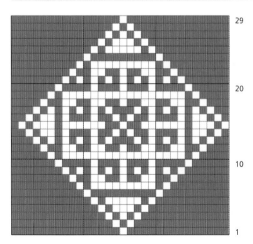

Rep 29 sts × 29 rows ⊛ 2

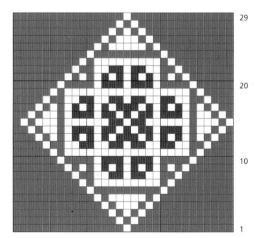

Rep 29 sts × 29 rows ⊛ 3

Rep 31 sts × 31 rows ⊛2

Rep 31 sts × 31 rows ⊛3

Rep 31 sts ×
31 rows ⊛2

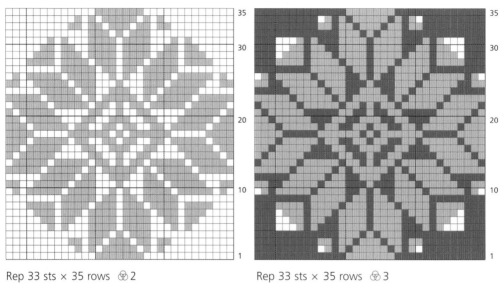

Rep 33 sts × 35 rows ✿2

Rep 33 sts × 35 rows ✿3

Rep 33 sts × 34 rows ✿2 ▷

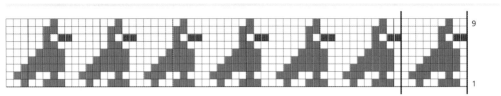

Rep 9 sts × 9 rows ⊗ 3

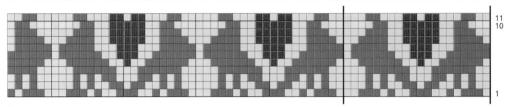

Rep 20 sts × 11 rows ⊗ 4

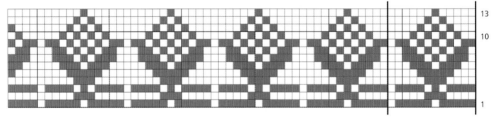

Rep 12 sts × 13 rows ⊗ 2

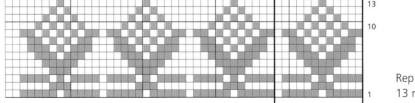

Rep 12 sts ×
13 rows ⊗ 3

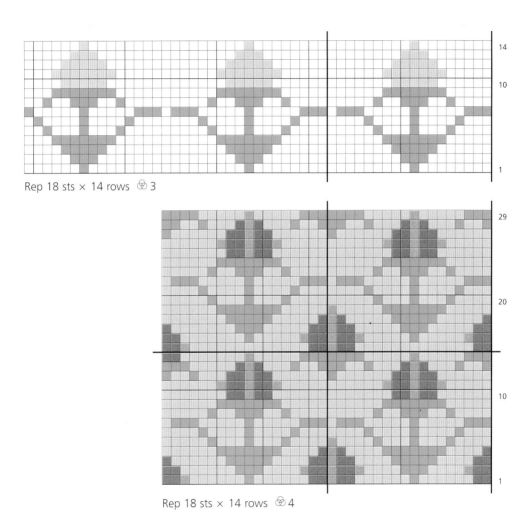

Rep 18 sts × 14 rows ⊛ 3

Rep 18 sts × 14 rows ⊛ 4

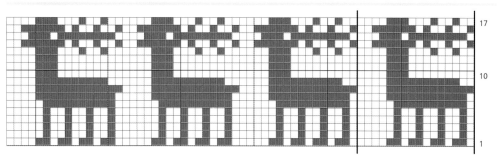

Rep 16 sts × 17 rows ✿ 2

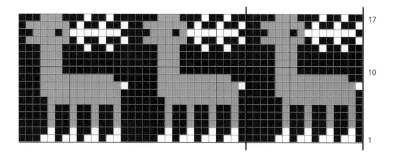

Rep 16 sts ×
17 rows ✿ 3

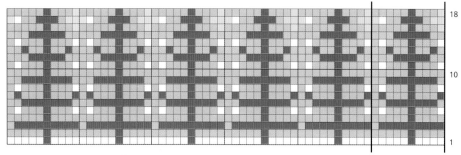

Rep 10 sts × 18 rows ✿ 4

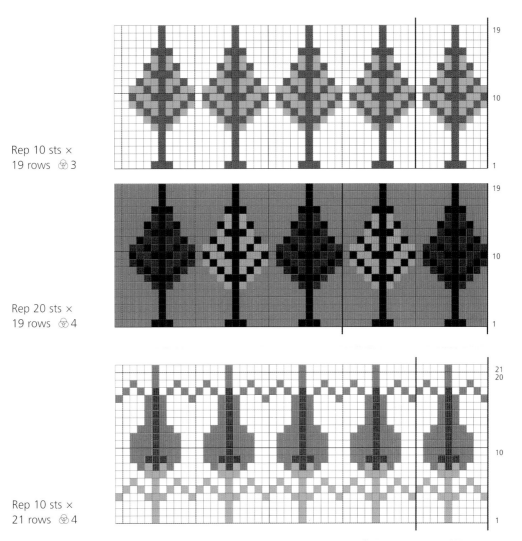

Rep 10 sts ×
19 rows ⊛ 3

Rep 20 sts ×
19 rows ⊛ 4

Rep 10 sts ×
21 rows ⊛ 4

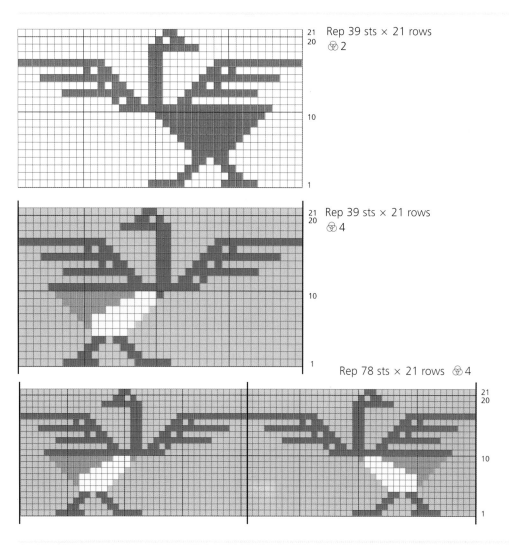

Rep 39 sts × 21 rows
🔘 2

Rep 39 sts × 21 rows
🔘 4

Rep 78 sts × 21 rows 🔘 4

142

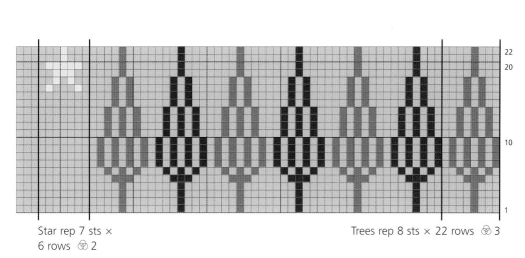

Star rep 7 sts ×
6 rows ⊛ 2

Trees rep 8 sts × 22 rows ⊛ 3

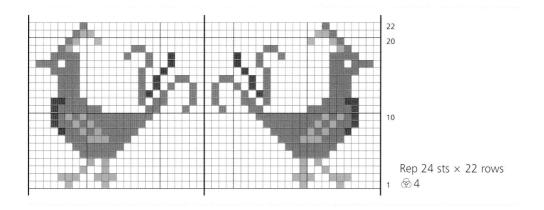

Rep 24 sts × 22 rows
⊛ 4

143

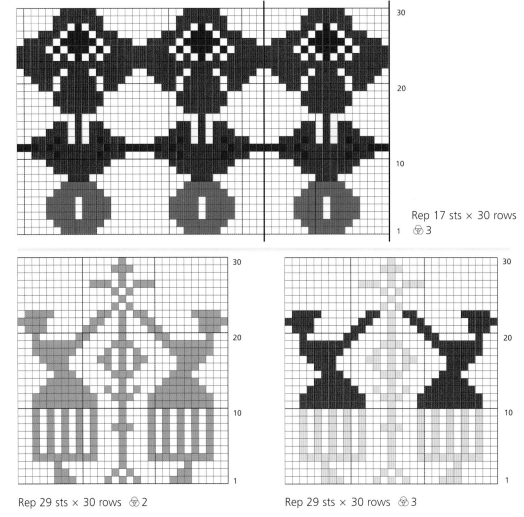

Rep 17 sts × 30 rows
🌼 3

Rep 29 sts × 30 rows 🌼 2

Rep 29 sts × 30 rows 🌼 3

Rep 35 sts × 32 rows
⊛ 2

Rep 39 sts × 31 rows
⊛ 2

Lapland

Lapland has a distinctive knitting style all of its own. Often the main color is worked with alternate stitches in a second color which changes on the next round or row. Traditionally the palette is limited to bright blue, red and occasionally gold on a cream background.

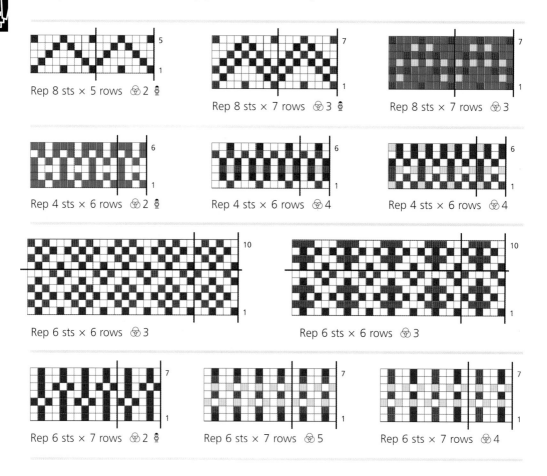

Rep 8 sts × 5 rows   2

Rep 8 sts × 7 rows   3

Rep 8 sts × 7 rows   3

Rep 4 sts × 6 rows   2

Rep 4 sts × 6 rows   4

Rep 4 sts × 6 rows   4

Rep 6 sts × 6 rows   3

Rep 6 sts × 6 rows   3

Rep 6 sts × 7 rows   2

Rep 6 sts × 7 rows   5

Rep 6 sts × 7 rows   4

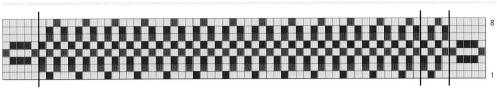

Rep 4 sts × 8 rows ⊛3 ⛄

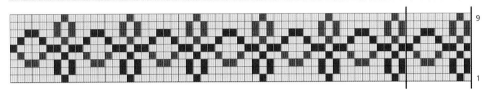

Rep 9 sts × 9 rows ⊛3 ⛄

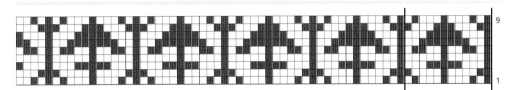

Rep 12 sts × 9 rows ⊛2 ⛄

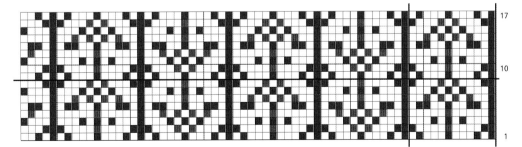

Rep 12 sts × 8 rows ⊛3 ⛄

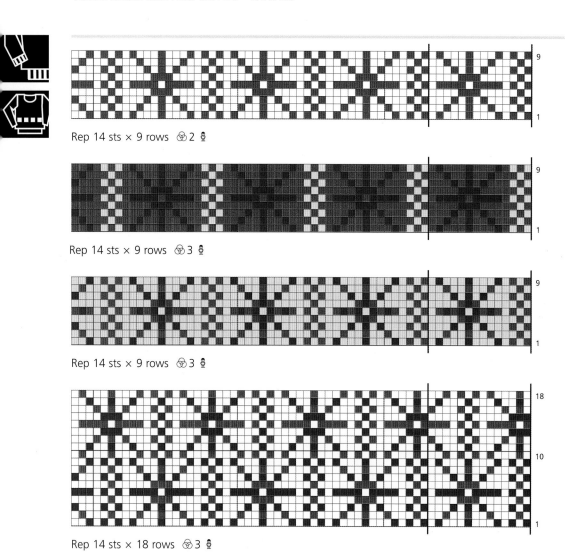

Rep 14 sts × 9 rows 2

Rep 14 sts × 9 rows 3

Rep 14 sts × 9 rows 3

Rep 14 sts × 18 rows 3

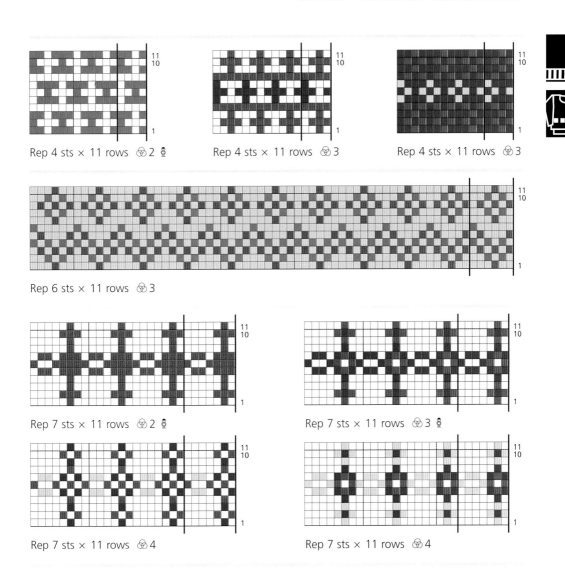

Rep 4 sts × 11 rows ⊛2 ⚇

Rep 4 sts × 11 rows ⊛3

Rep 4 sts × 11 rows ⊛3

Rep 6 sts × 11 rows ⊛3

Rep 7 sts × 11 rows ⊛2 ⚇

Rep 7 sts × 11 rows ⊛3 ⚇

Rep 7 sts × 11 rows ⊛4

Rep 7 sts × 11 rows ⊛4

149

Rep 10 sts × 11 rows
⊛ 2

Rep 10 sts × 11 rows ⊛ 4

Rep 10 sts × 11 rows
⊛ 4

Rep 12 sts × 11 rows ⊛ 4

Rep 6 sts × 11 rows ⊛ 4

Rep 28 sts × 14 rows ⊛ 2

Rep 15 sts × 14 rows
⊛ 3

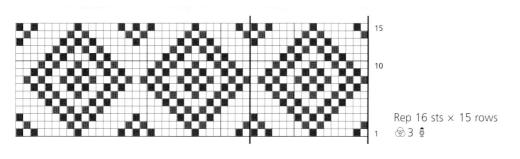

Rep 16 sts × 15 rows
⊛ 3 ⚇

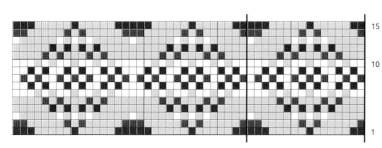

Rep 16 sts × 15 rows
⊛ 5

Rep 10 sts × 20 rows ⊛ 4

151

Western Europe

France, Germany and Austria all have a very strong knitting tradition often influenced by the embroidery and quilt making of the home. Strong geometric shapes, particularly squares, diamonds, triangles, and crosses are often accompanied by surface embroidery influenced by the flora and fauna in the area. In Holland, the designs tend to be very simlar but more sombre with very little embroidery. In the mountainous areas, strong tones in natural colors are favored with red often being used as a decorative highlight. The further north and west in the region, the more gray and muted the colors become, with subtle tones being used together.

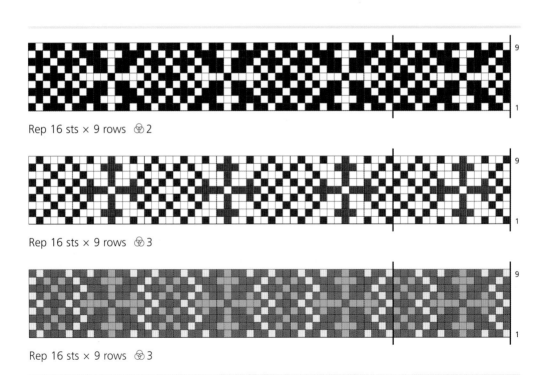

Rep 16 sts × 9 rows   ✿2

Rep 16 sts × 9 rows   ✿3

Rep 16 sts × 9 rows   ✿3

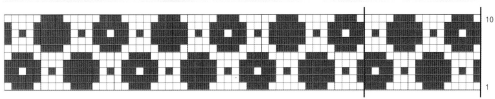

Rep 16 sts × 10 rows 2

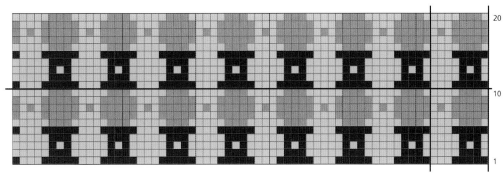

Rep 8 sts × 10 rows 3

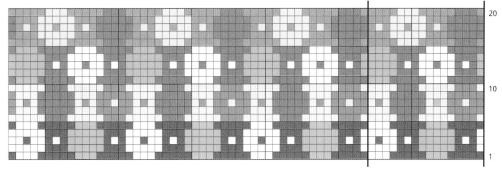

Rep 16 sts × 20 rows 9

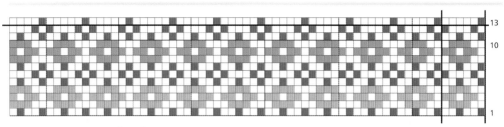

Rep 6 sts × 12 rows ⊛ 4 ⚇

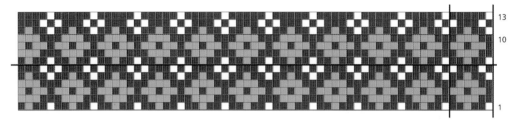

Rep 6 sts × 6 rows ⊛ 3 ⚇

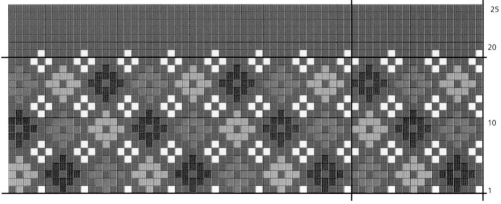

Rep 18 sts × 18 rows ⊛ 5 ⚇

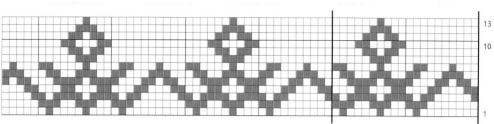

Rep 20 sts × 13 rows ⊛ 2

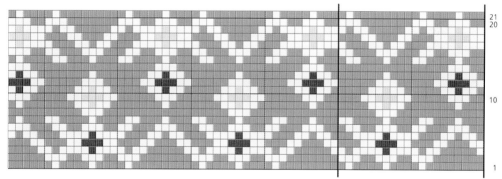

Rep 20 sts × 21 rows ⊛ 4

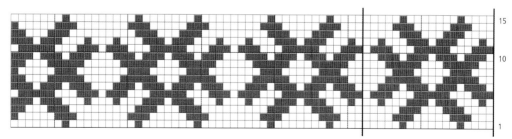

Rep 18 sts × 15 rows ⊛ 2

Rep 10 sts × 27 rows ❀ 2

Rep 10 sts × 27 rows ❀ 5

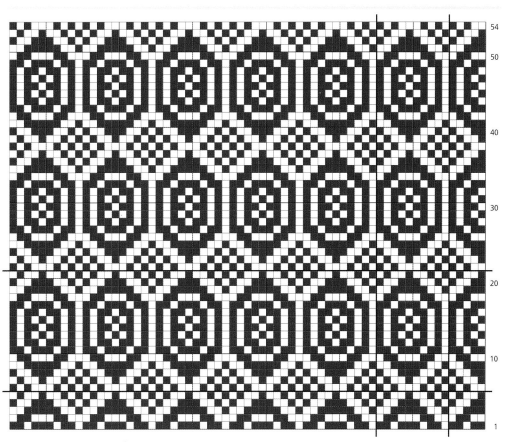

Rep 10 sts × 16 rows ⊗ 2

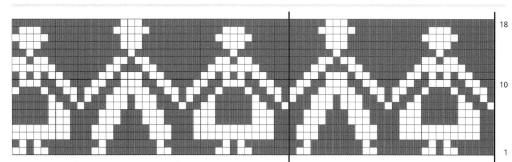

Rep 28 sts × 18 rows ⊛2 🯄

Rep 32 sts × 18 rows ⊛ 3

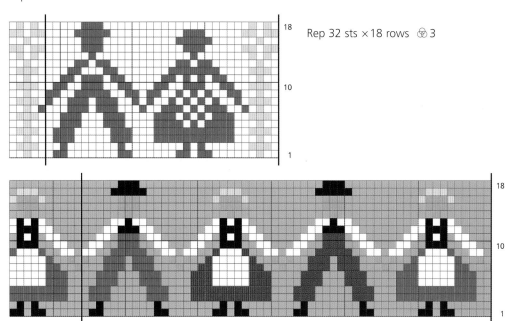

Rep 56 sts × 18 rows ⊛9 🯄

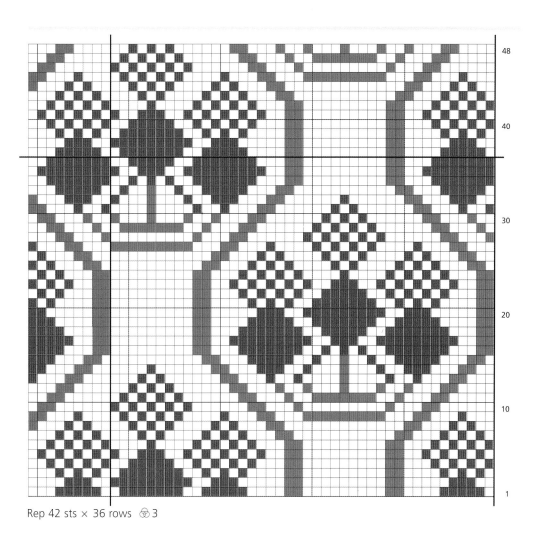

Rep 42 sts × 36 rows ⊛ 3

Eastern Europe

The key to recognizing the knitting tradition of Eastern Europe is the use of small patterns over the entire knitted fabric, with a smaller repeat being used rather than plain areas of stockinette (stocking) stitch. A dark brown, that is almost black, is often used with natural blues and reds achieved by using woad and madder. Cream and golds are also popular background colors. The continuous stranding of two or three colors creates a dense and warm protective fabric. To create the Eastern European look, combine a two or three row repeat from this, or the Fair Isle chapter, with a deep star or diamond edging from the Scandinavian chapter in strong contrasting colors.

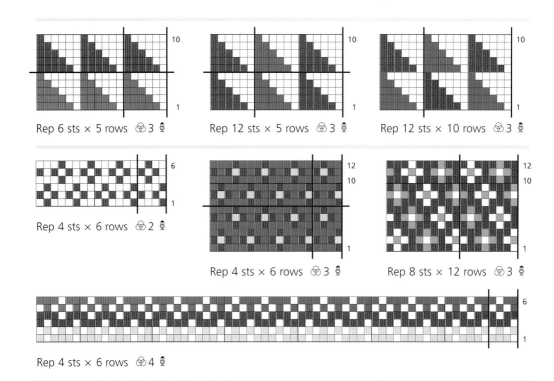

Rep 6 sts × 5 rows ⊛ 3 ⚲

Rep 12 sts × 5 rows ⊛ 3 ⚲

Rep 12 sts × 10 rows ⊛ 3 ⚲

Rep 4 sts × 6 rows ⊛ 2 ⚲

Rep 4 sts × 6 rows ⊛ 3 ⚲

Rep 8 sts × 12 rows ⊛ 3 ⚲

Rep 4 sts × 6 rows ⊛ 4 ⚲

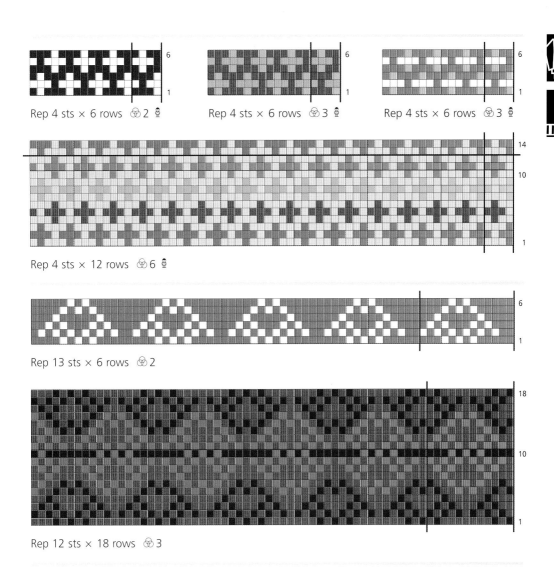

Rep 4 sts × 6 rows ⊛2 🎎

Rep 4 sts × 6 rows ⊛3 🎎

Rep 4 sts × 6 rows ⊛3 🎎

Rep 4 sts × 12 rows ⊛6 🎎

Rep 13 sts × 6 rows ⊛2

Rep 12 sts × 18 rows ⊛3

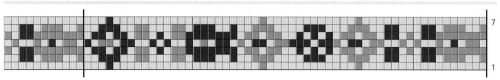

Rep 55 sts × 7 rows ✾3 👤

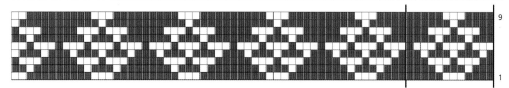

Rep 12 sts × 9 rows ✾2

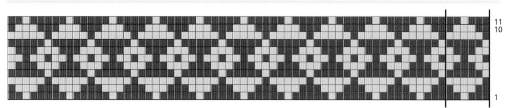

Rep 6 sts × 11 rows ✾2 👤

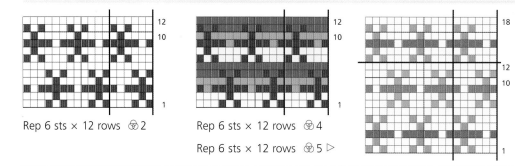

Rep 6 sts × 12 rows ✾2

Rep 6 sts × 12 rows ✾4

Rep 6 sts × 12 rows ✾5 ▷

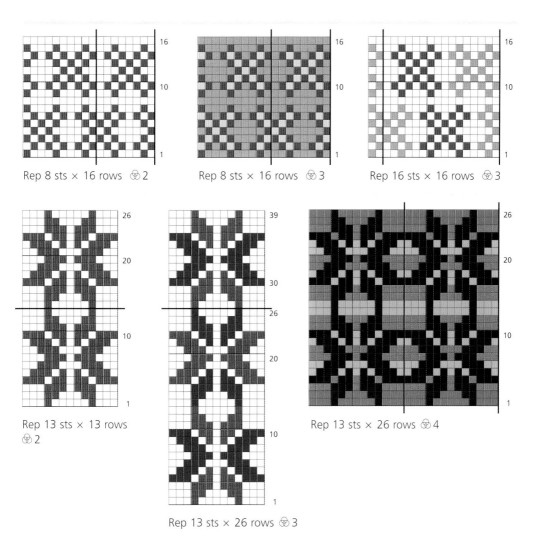

Rep 8 sts × 16 rows ⊛ 2

Rep 8 sts × 16 rows ⊛ 3

Rep 16 sts × 16 rows ⊛ 3

Rep 13 sts × 13 rows
⊛ 2

Rep 13 sts × 26 rows ⊛ 4

Rep 13 sts × 26 rows ⊛ 3

Rep 18 sts × 18 rows ⊛ 2

Rep 18 sts × 18 rows ⊛ 3

Rep 18 sts × 18 rows ⊛ 4

Rep 18 sts × 18 rows ⊛ 4

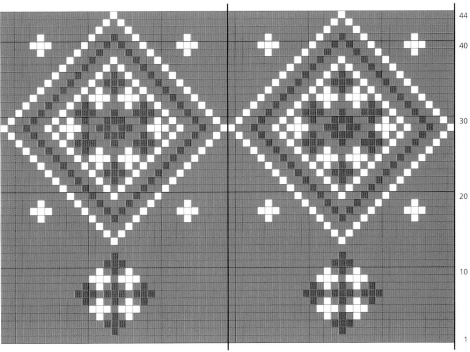

Rep 31 sts × 44 rows ⊛ 3

Around the Mediterranean Sea

Italy and southern France have a strong history of lace knitting. However, as you travel east and south around the Mediterranean Sea the color knitting tradition favors smaller square and diamond repeat patterns which are used to trim and highlight, rather than as an overall pattern. The shapes on east and north African fabrics resemble the tradition of South America with bright colors that change frequently and stylized representations of the local fauna and flora. Golds, silvers, pale blues and pinks are popular colors, as is a particularly bilious green.

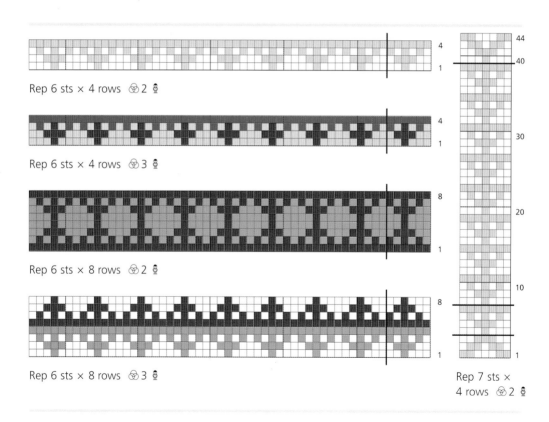

Rep 6 sts × 4 rows ⊛2 ⦶

Rep 6 sts × 4 rows ⊛3 ⦶

Rep 6 sts × 8 rows ⊛2 ⦶

Rep 6 sts × 8 rows ⊛3 ⦶

Rep 7 sts ×
4 rows ⊛2 ⦶

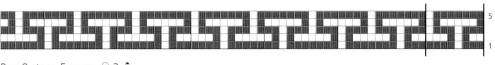

Rep 8 sts × 5 rows ⊛ 2 🧍

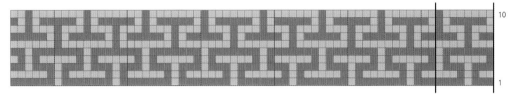

Rep 8 sts × 10 rows ⊛ 2 🧍

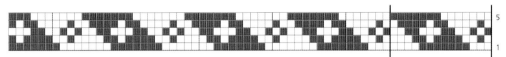

Rep 14 sts × 5 rows ⊛ 2 🧍

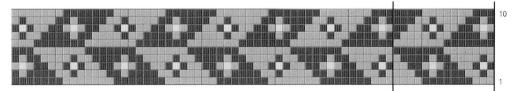

Rep 14 sts × 10 rows ⊛ 3 🧍

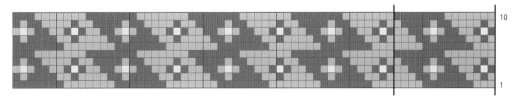

Rep 14 sts × 10 rows ⊛ 3 🧍

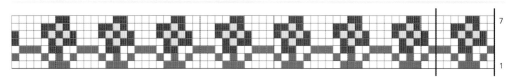

Rep 8 sts × 7 rows ⊛ 4 ⦾

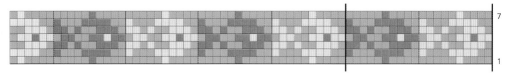

Rep 20 sts × 7 rows ⊛ 3 ⦾

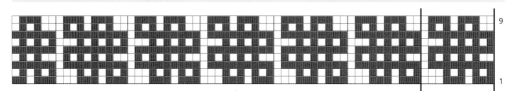

Rep 10 sts × 9 rows ⊛ 2

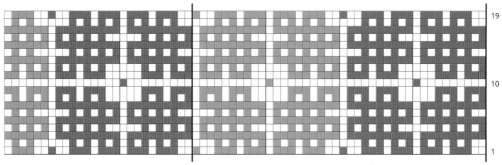

Rep 40 sts × 19 rows ⊛ 3 ⦾

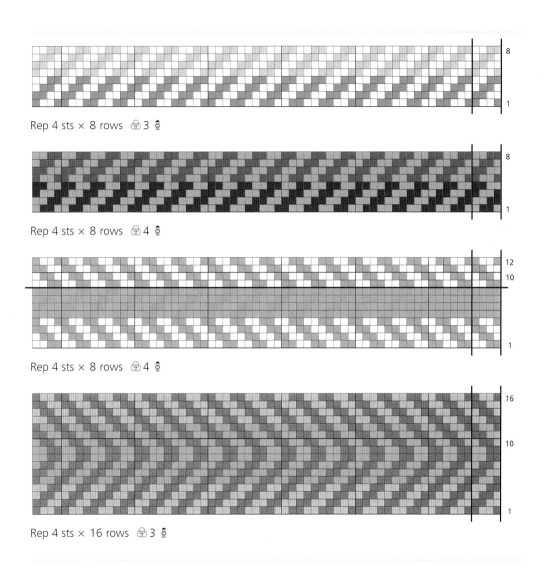

Rep 4 sts × 8 rows 🌐 3 👤

Rep 4 sts × 8 rows 🌐 4 👤

Rep 4 sts × 8 rows 🌐 4 👤

Rep 4 sts × 16 rows 🌐 3 👤

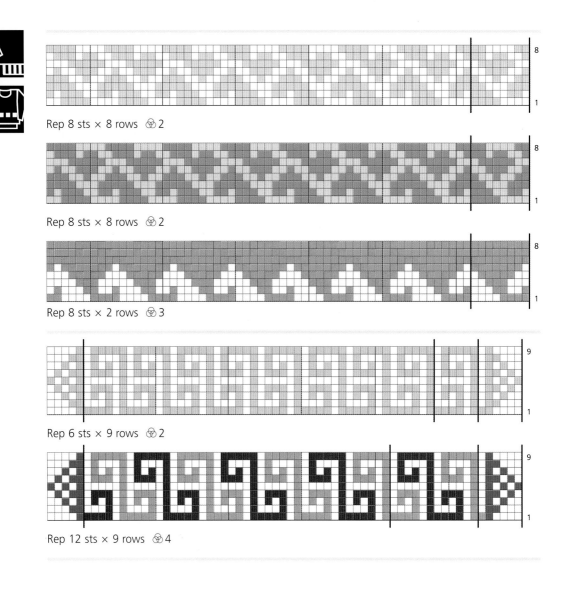

Rep 8 sts × 8 rows ✥ 2

Rep 8 sts × 8 rows ✥ 2

Rep 8 sts × 2 rows ✥ 3

Rep 6 sts × 9 rows ✥ 2

Rep 12 sts × 9 rows ✥ 4

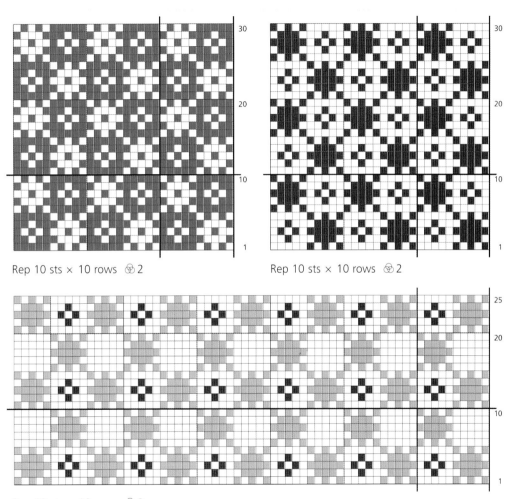

Rep 10 sts × 10 rows ✪ 2

Rep 10 sts × 10 rows ✪ 2

Rep 10 sts × 10 rows ✪ 3

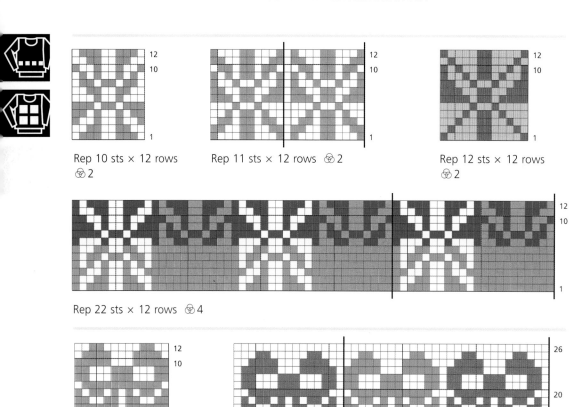

Rep 10 sts × 12 rows ⊛2

Rep 11 sts × 12 rows ⊛2

Rep 12 sts × 12 rows ⊛2

Rep 22 sts × 12 rows ⊛4

Rep 13 sts × 12 rows ⊛2 ⚱

Rep 28 sts × 26 rows ⊛3 ⚱ ▷

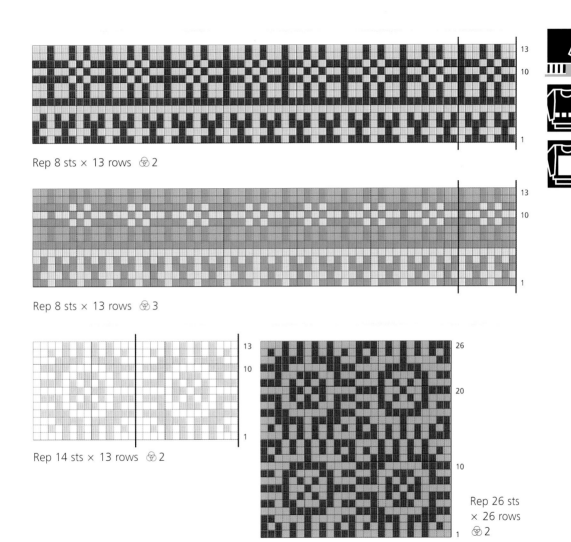

Rep 8 sts × 13 rows ⊛ 2

Rep 8 sts × 13 rows ⊛ 3

Rep 14 sts × 13 rows ⊛ 2

Rep 26 sts
× 26 rows
⊛ 2

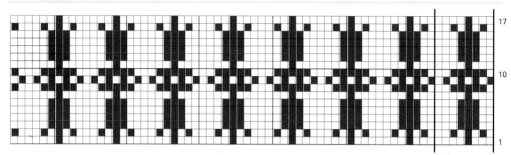

Rep 8 sts × 17 rows ⊛ 2 🕯

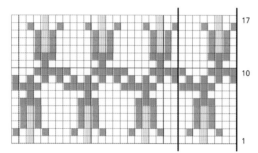

Rep 8 sts × 17 rows ⊛ 4 🕯

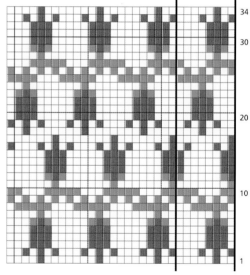

Rep 8 sts × 34 rows ⊛ 3

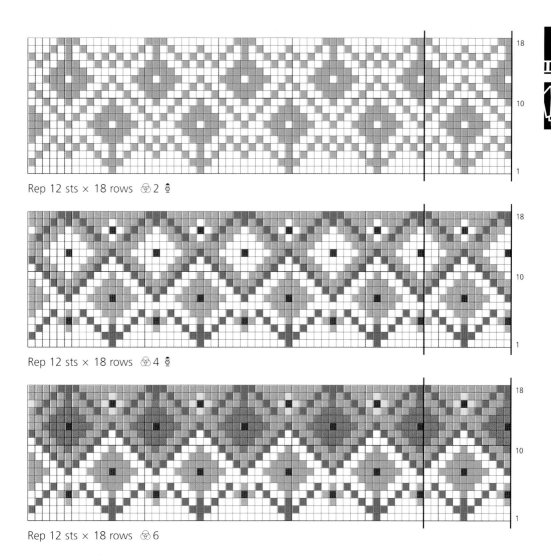

Rep 12 sts × 18 rows ⊛ 2 👤

Rep 12 sts × 18 rows ⊛ 4 👤

Rep 12 sts × 18 rows ⊛ 6

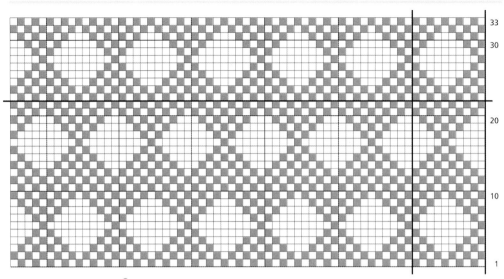

33
30

20

10

1

Rep 10 sts × 22 rows ⊛2

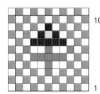

10

1

11 sts × 11
rows ⊛4
See above.

11 sts × 11
rows ⊛4
See above.

11 sts × 11
rows ⊛5
See above.

11 sts × 11
rows ⊛3
See above.

11 sts × 11
rows ⊛5
See above.

Rep 9 sts ×
15 rows ✾ 3

Rep 9 sts ×
30 rows ✾ 5

Rep 9 sts ×
19 rows ✾ 3

Rep 9 sts ×
19 rows ✾ 4

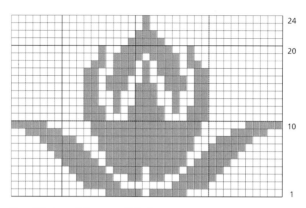

Rep 37 sts × 24 rows ⊛2 🕯

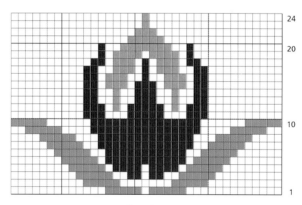

Rep 37 sts × 24 rows ⊛4 🕯

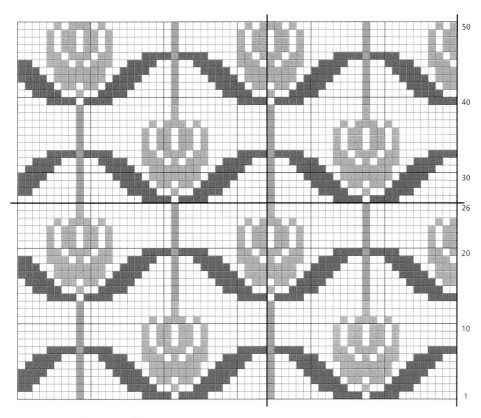

Rep 26 sts × 26 rows 3

63
60

50

40

34
30

20

10

1

Rep 16 sts × 34 rows ⊛ 3

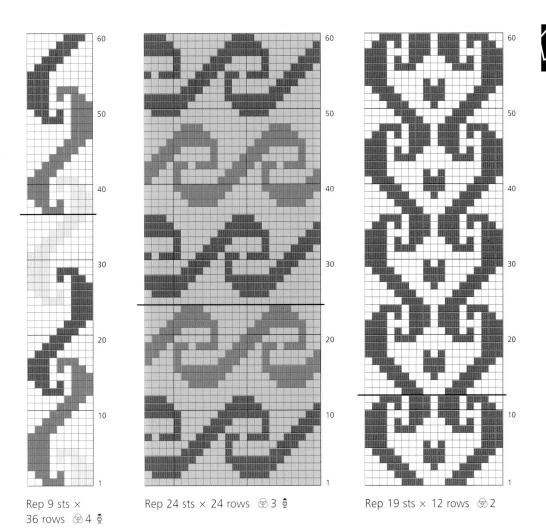

Rep 9 sts ×
36 rows ⊛4 ⚇

Rep 24 sts × 24 rows ⊛3 ⚇

Rep 19 sts × 12 rows ⊛2

Asia

There isn't a strong tradition of Asian knitting and the designs are quite hard to find. However, there is a tendency for small repeat patterns in the colors of Chinese pottery and local spices. Some of the patterns are traditional decorative motifs possibly adapted by travelers for knitting. Many of the other designs are similar to those in other chapters but it is the colors and the repetition of motif that give the area its knitting character. This is very different from today's knitting which favors strong colors and often large, bold, figurative motifs.

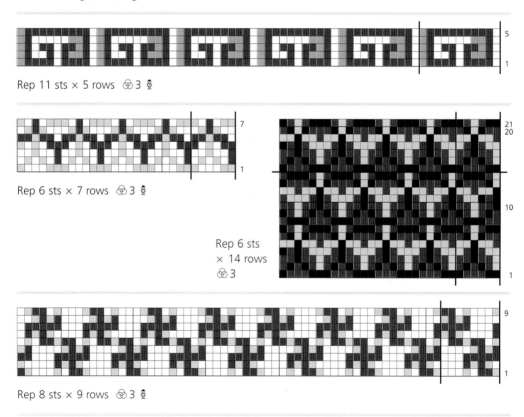

Rep 11 sts × 5 rows ⊛3 🕯

Rep 6 sts × 7 rows ⊛3 🕯

Rep 6 sts
× 14 rows
⊛3

Rep 8 sts × 9 rows ⊛3 🕯

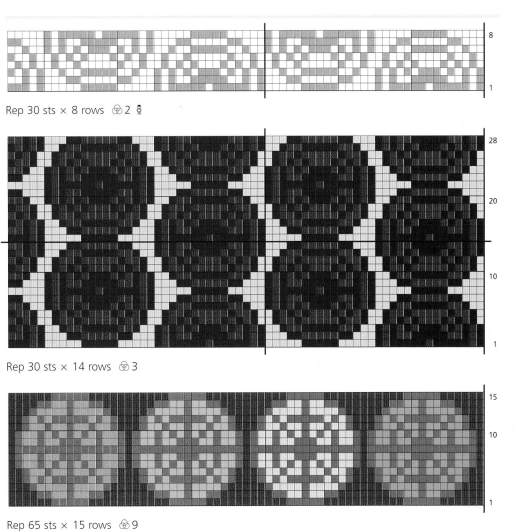

Rep 30 sts × 8 rows ⊛ 2

Rep 30 sts × 14 rows ⊛ 3

Rep 65 sts × 15 rows ⊛ 9

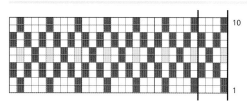

Rep 4 sts × 10 rows ⊗ 3

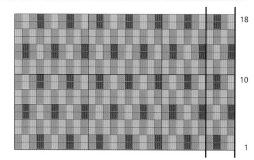

Rep 4 sts × 10 rows ⊗ 3

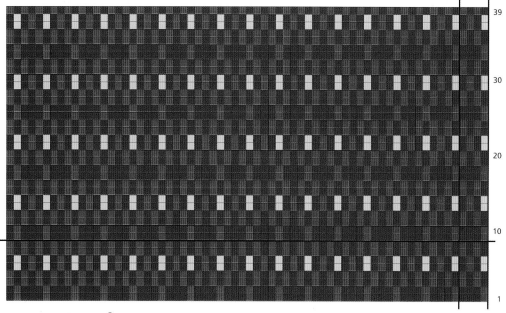

Rep 4 sts × 8 rows ⊗ 3

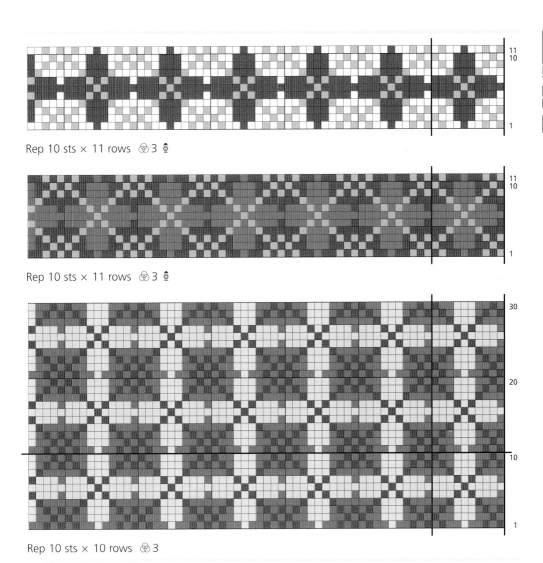

Rep 10 sts × 11 rows ⊛ 3 ⚱

Rep 10 sts × 11 rows ⊛ 3 ⚱

Rep 10 sts × 10 rows ⊛ 3

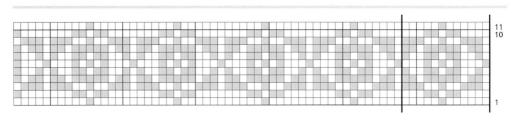

Rep 12 sts × 11 rows ⊛2 ⚲

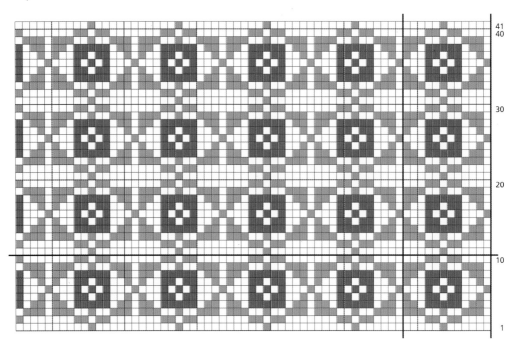

Rep 12 sts × 10 rows ⊛3

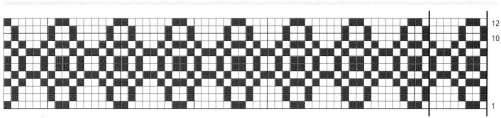

Rep 8 sts × 12 rows ✾ 3 ♟

Rep 20 sts × 12 rows ✾ 2

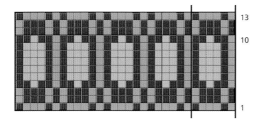

Rep 6 sts × 13 rows ✾ 3

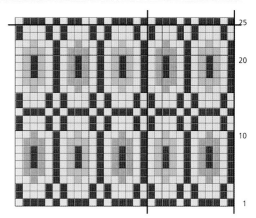

Rep 12 sts × 24 rows ✾ 4

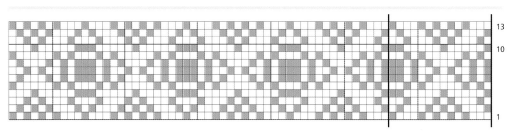

Rep 14 sts × 13 rows ⊗ 2

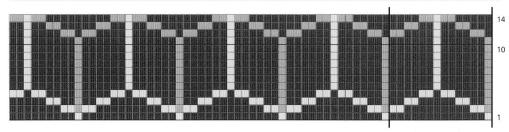

Rep 14 sts × 14 rows ⊗ 3 ⚱

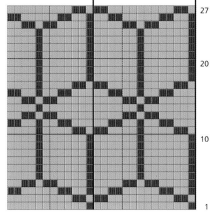

Rep 14 sts
× 27 rows
⊗ 2

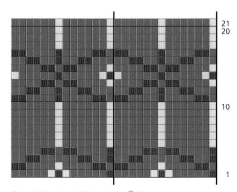

Rep 14 sts × 21 rows ⊗ 3
See left for pattern continuation.

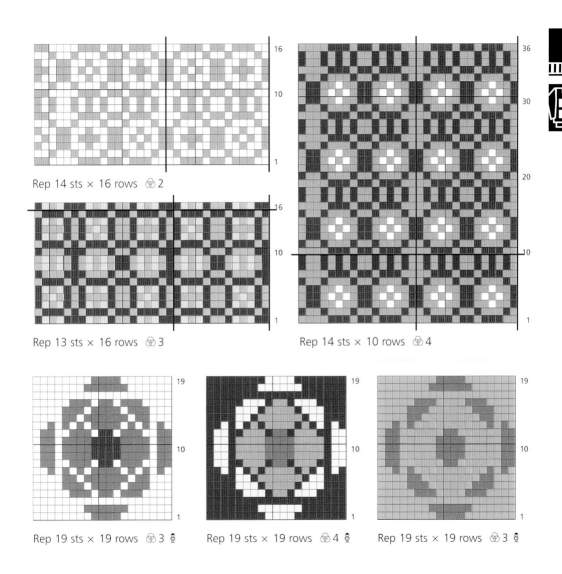

Rep 14 sts × 16 rows ⊛ 2

Rep 13 sts × 16 rows ⊛ 3

Rep 14 sts × 10 rows ⊛ 4

Rep 19 sts × 19 rows ⊛ 3 ⚓

Rep 19 sts × 19 rows ⊛ 4 ⚓

Rep 19 sts × 19 rows ⊛ 3 ⚓

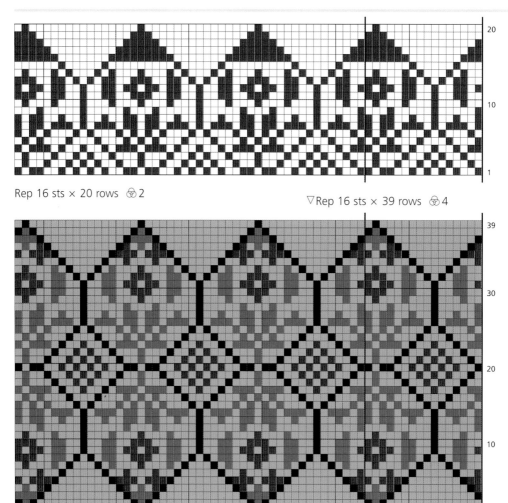

Rep 16 sts × 20 rows ⊛2

▽Rep 16 sts × 39 rows ⊛4

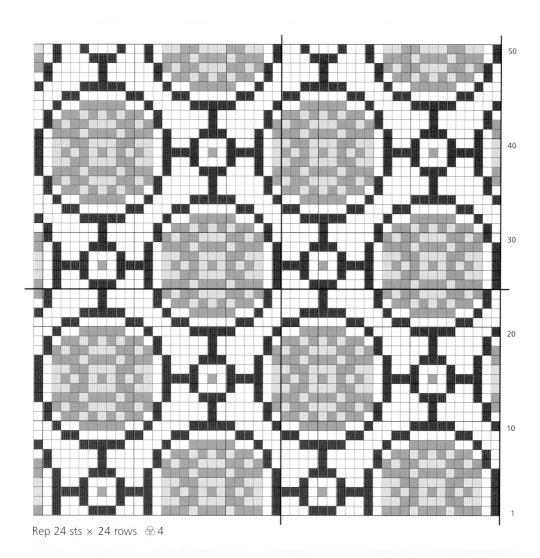

Rep 24 sts × 24 rows ⊛ 4

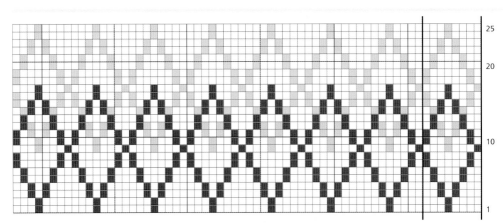

Rep 8 sts × 25 rows ⊛3 ⛟

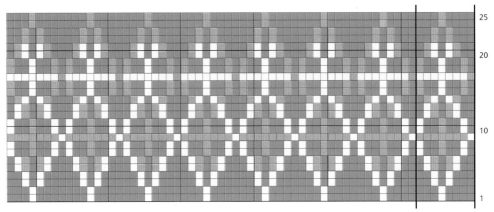

Rep 8 sts × 25 rows ⊛3 ⛟

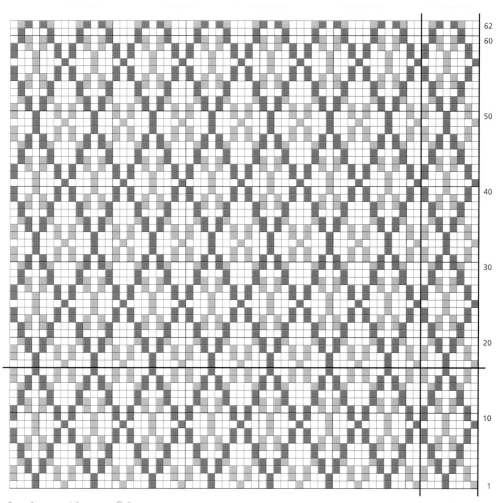

Rep 8 sts × 16 rows ⊛ 3

South America

The countries of South America have a strong knitting tradition using very bright, almost luminous colors, mixed in improbable combinations in the most luscious knitwear. Again, many of the motifs in the Fair Isle section are found in South American designs but in brighter hues, with regular changes of color.

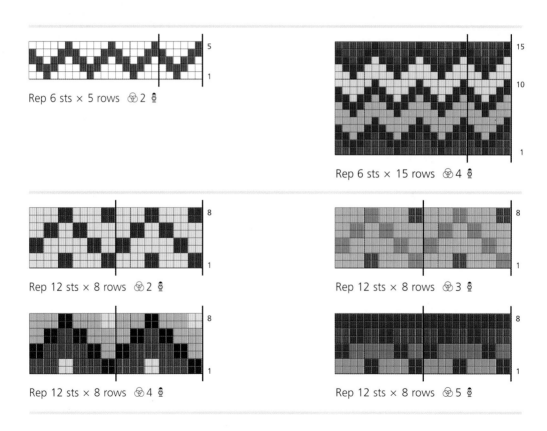

Rep 6 sts × 5 rows ❀2 ☖

Rep 6 sts × 15 rows ❀4 ☖

Rep 12 sts × 8 rows ❀2 ☖

Rep 12 sts × 8 rows ❀3 ☖

Rep 12 sts × 8 rows ❀4 ☖

Rep 12 sts × 8 rows ❀5 ☖

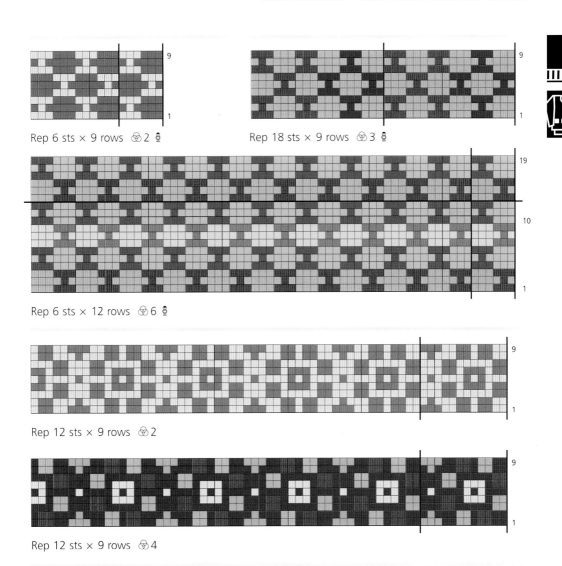

Rep 6 sts × 9 rows ⊛ 2 ⚇

Rep 18 sts × 9 rows ⊛ 3 ⚇

Rep 6 sts × 12 rows ⊛ 6 ⚇

Rep 12 sts × 9 rows ⊛ 2

Rep 12 sts × 9 rows ⊛ 4

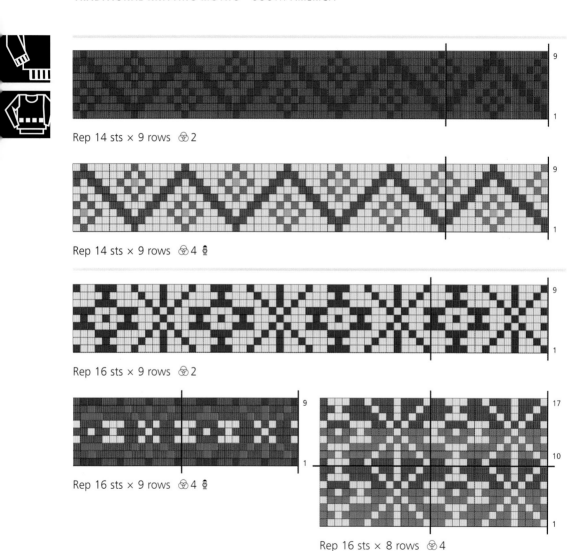

Rep 14 sts × 9 rows ⊛ 2

Rep 14 sts × 9 rows ⊛ 4 👤

Rep 16 sts × 9 rows ⊛ 2

Rep 16 sts × 9 rows ⊛ 4 👤

Rep 16 sts × 8 rows ⊛ 4

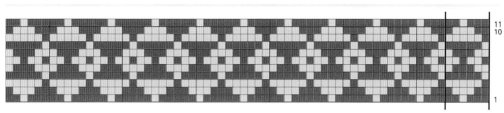

Rep 6 sts × 11 rows ⊛ 2

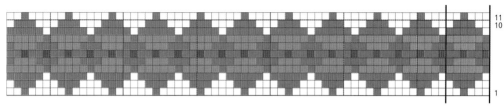

Rep 6 sts × 11 rows ⊛ 4

Rep 14 sts × 11 rows ⊛ 3

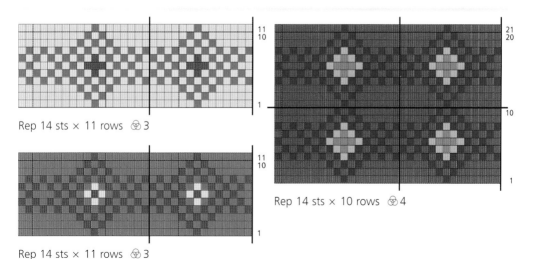

Rep 14 sts × 10 rows ⊛ 4

Rep 14 sts × 11 rows ⊛ 3

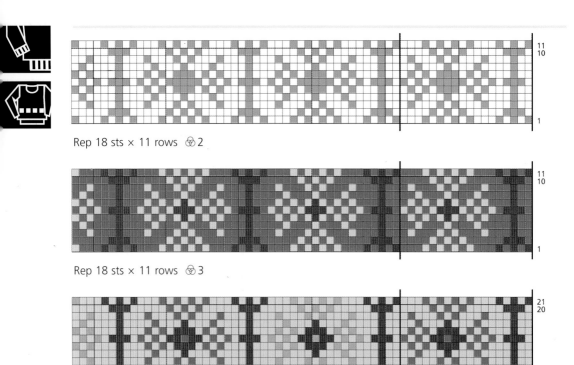

Rep 18 sts × 11 rows ⊗2

Rep 18 sts × 11 rows ⊗3

Rep 18 sts × 10 rows ⊗4

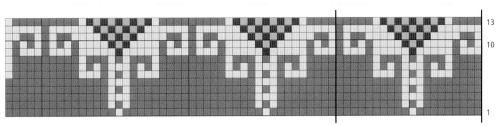

Rep 20 sts × 13 rows ⊛ 4

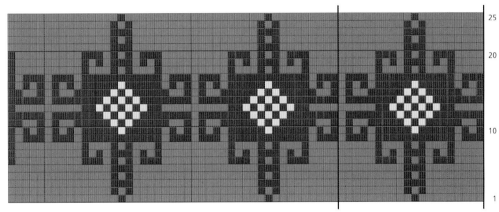

Rep 20 sts × 25 rows ⊛ 3

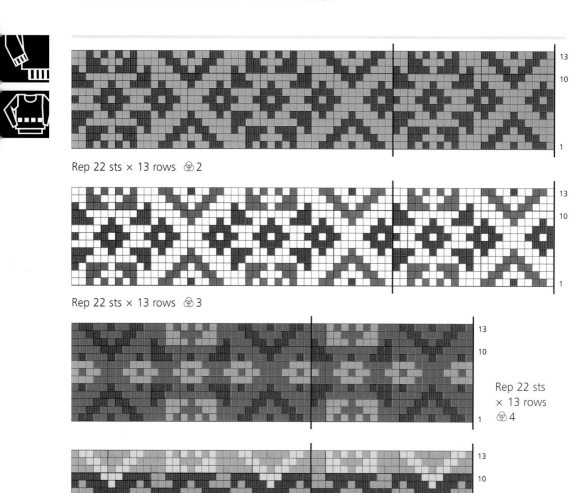

Rep 22 sts × 13 rows ⊛ 2

Rep 22 sts × 13 rows ⊛ 3

Rep 22 sts
× 13 rows
⊛ 4

Rep 22 sts
× 13 rows
⊛ 4

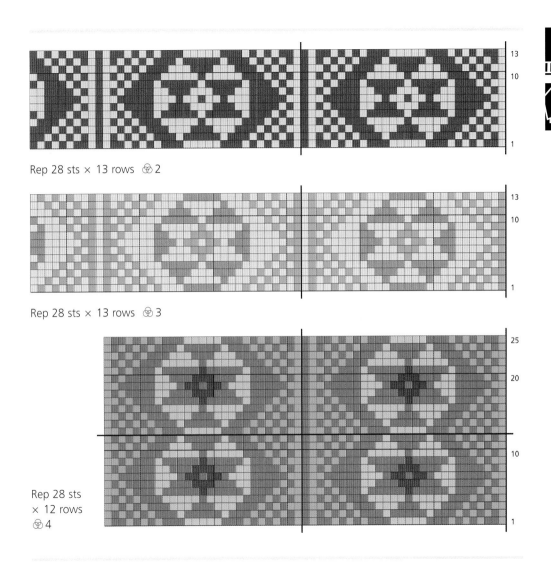

Rep 28 sts × 13 rows ⊛ 2

Rep 28 sts × 13 rows ⊛ 3

Rep 28 sts × 12 rows ⊛ 4

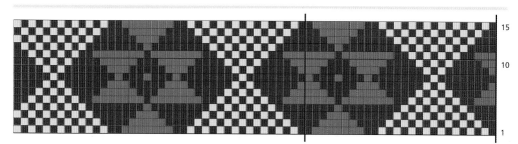

Rep 26 sts × 15 rows 3

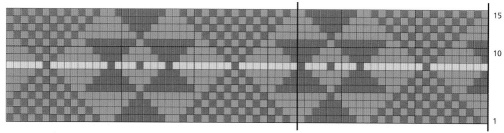

Rep 26 sts × 15 rows 4

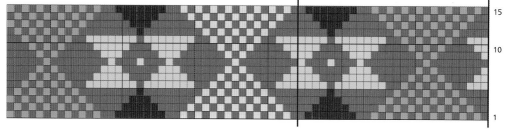

Rep 26 sts × 15 rows 5

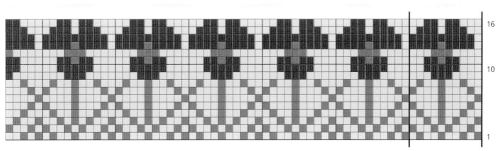

Rep 10 sts × 16 rows ⊛ 4 ⚇

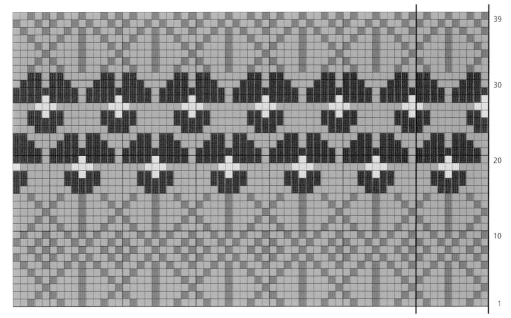

Rep 10 sts × 39 rows ⊛ 4

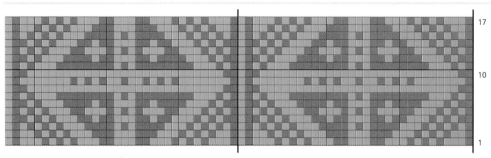

Rep 32 sts × 17 rows ⊛ 2

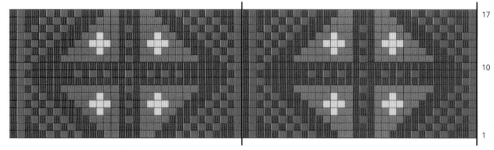

Rep 32 sts × 17 rows ⊛ 4

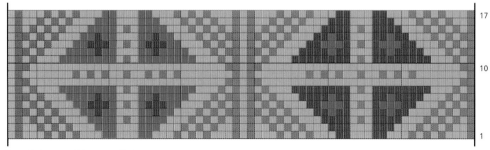

Rep 64 sts × 17 rows ⊛ 4

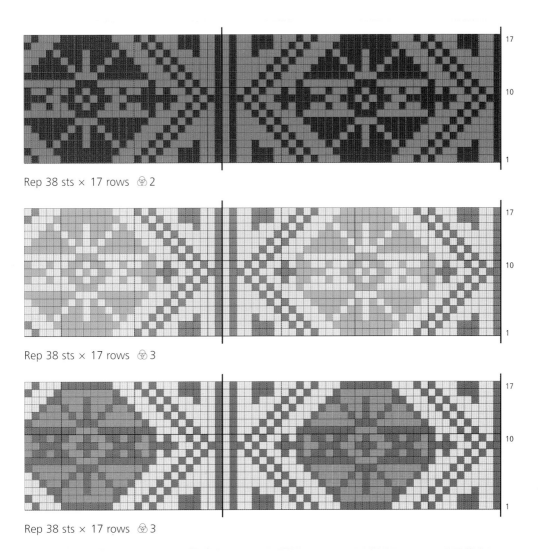

Rep 38 sts × 17 rows ⊛ 2

Rep 38 sts × 17 rows ⊛ 3

Rep 38 sts × 17 rows ⊛ 3

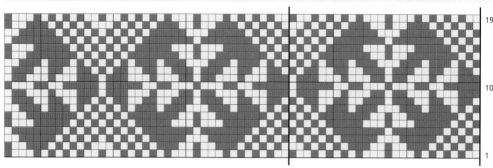

Rep 26 sts × 19 rows ⊛ 2

Rep 26 sts
× 18 rows
⊛ 3

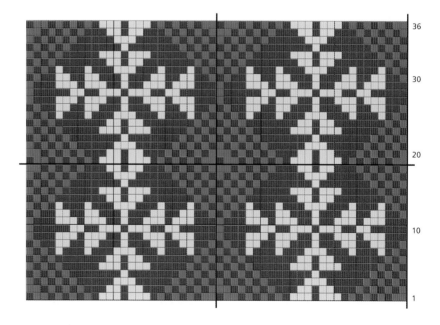

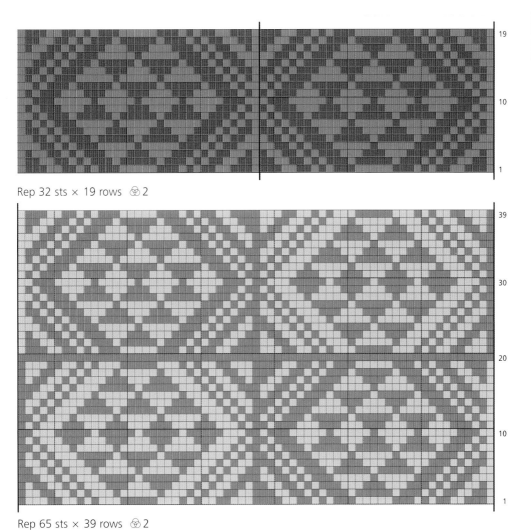

Rep 32 sts × 19 rows ⊛ 2

Rep 65 sts × 39 rows ⊛ 2

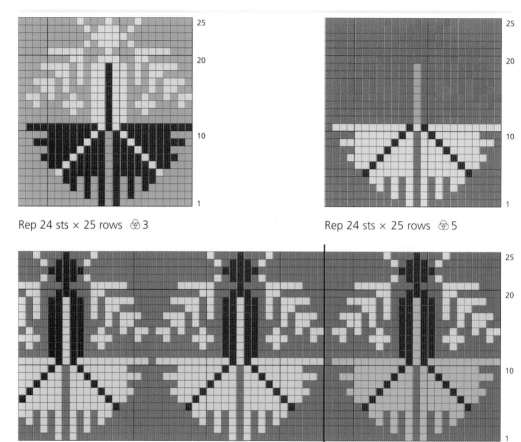

Rep 24 sts × 25 rows ⊛ 3

Rep 24 sts × 25 rows ⊛ 5

Rep 24 sts × 25 rows ⊛ 4

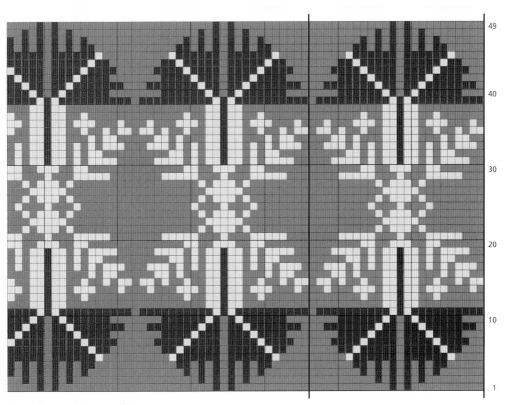

Rep 24 sts × 49 rows ⊛ 3

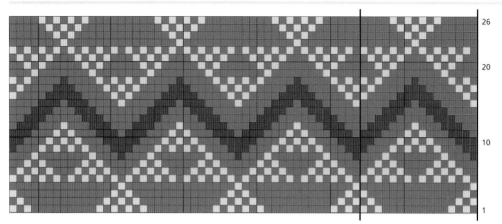

Rep 16 sts × 26 rows ⊛ 3

Rep 16 sts × 26 rows ⊛ 5

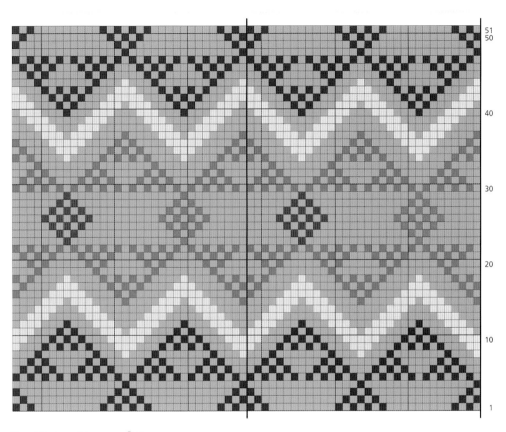

Rep 32 sts × 51 rows ⊛ 6

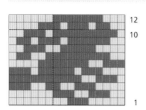

Rep 16 sts × 12 rows
🌑2 👤

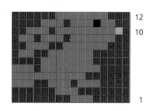

Rep 16 sts × 12 rows
🌑4 👤

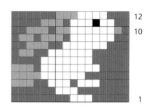

Rep 16 sts × 12 rows
🌑3 👤

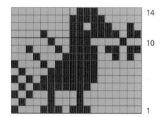

Rep 18 sts × 14 rows 🌑2 👤

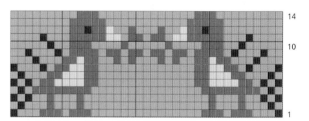

Rep 37 sts × 14 rows 🌑5 👤

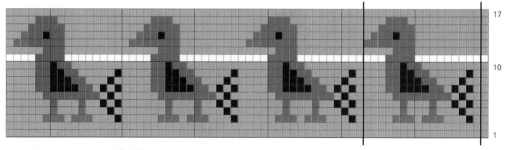

Rep 16 sts × 17 rows 🌑5 👤

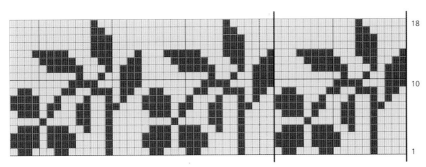

Rep 18 sts × 18 rows ⊛2 ⚇

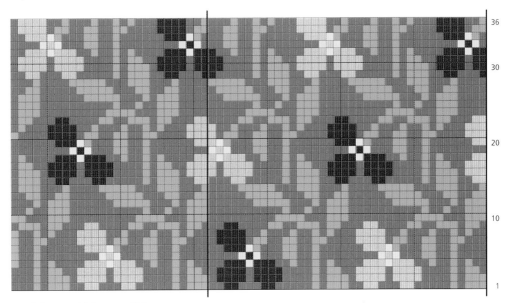

Rep 36 sts × 126 rows ⊛5

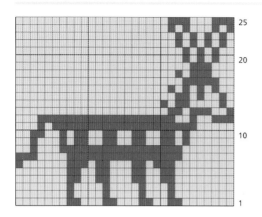

Rep 30 sts × 25 rows ✡ 2

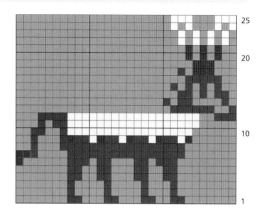

Rep 30 sts × 25 rows ✡ 4

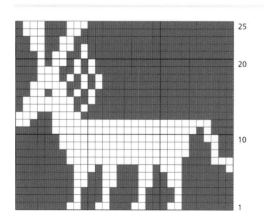

Rep 30 sts × 25 rows ✡ 2 ⚇

Rep 30 sts × 25 rows ✡ 3 ⚇

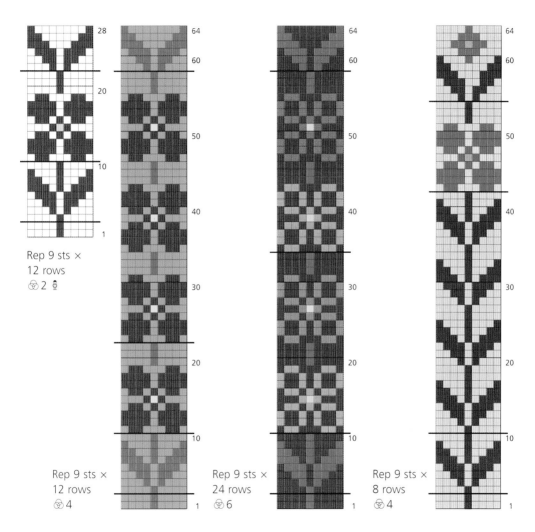

Rep 9 sts ×
12 rows
⊛2 ⚇

Rep 9 sts ×
12 rows
⊛4

Rep 9 sts ×
24 rows
⊛6

Rep 9 sts ×
8 rows
⊛4

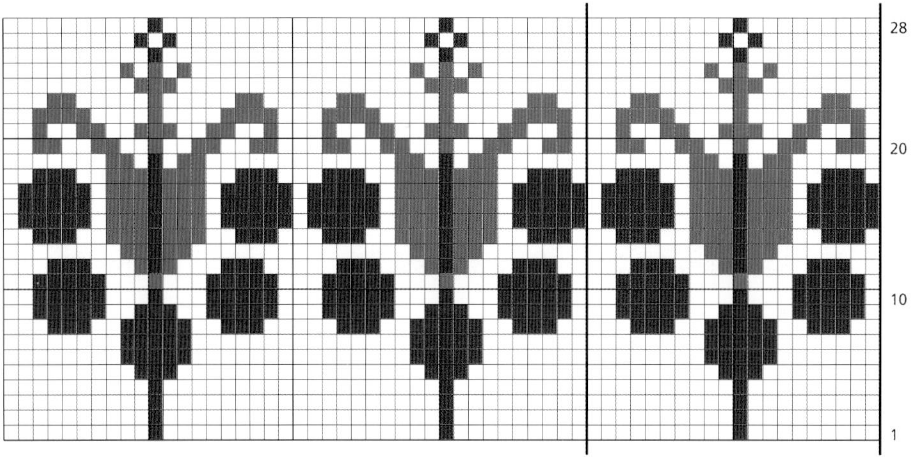

Rep 20 sts × 28 rows ⊛3

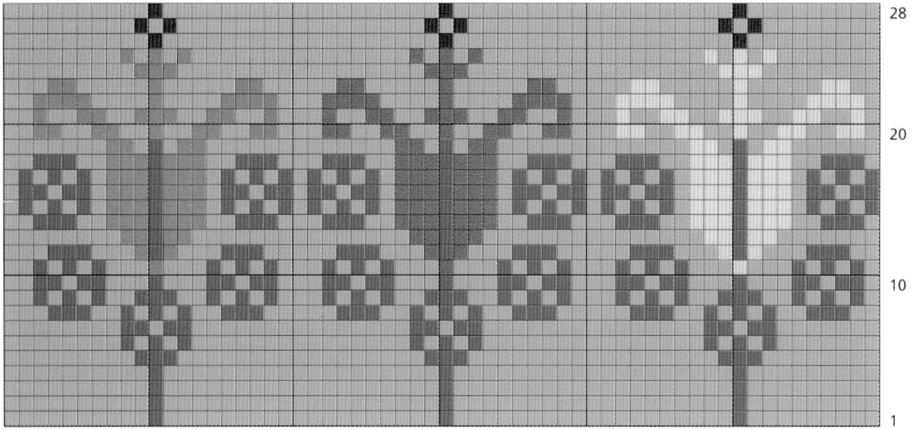

Rep 60 sts × 28 rows ⊛6

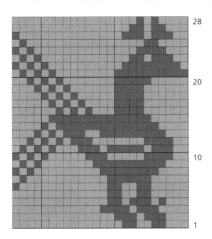

Rep 24 sts × 28 rows ⊛ 2

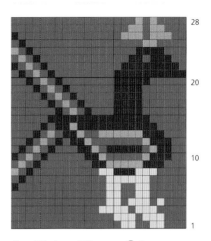

Rep 24 sts × 28 rows ⊛ 4

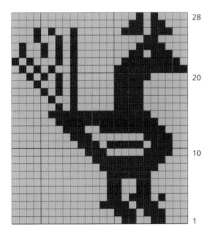

Rep 24 sts × 28 rows ⊛ 2

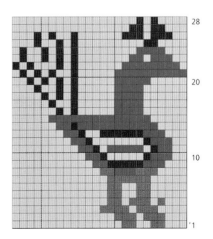

Rep 24 sts × 28 rows ⊛ 4

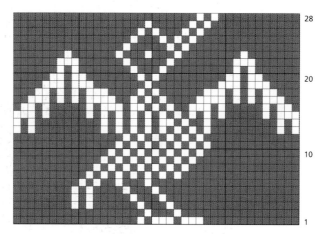

Rep 39 sts × 28 rows ⊛ 2

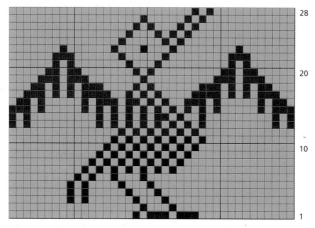

Rep 39 sts × 28 rows ⊛ 3

Traditional
pictorial motifs

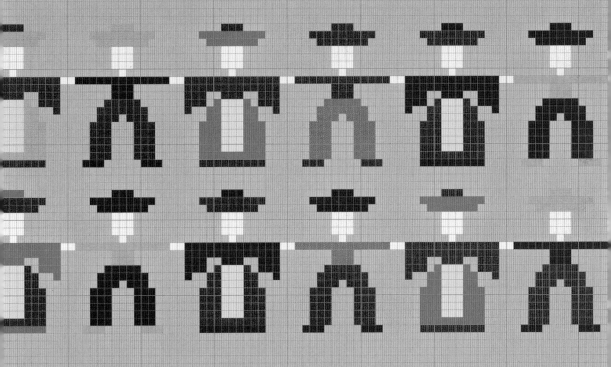

Native America

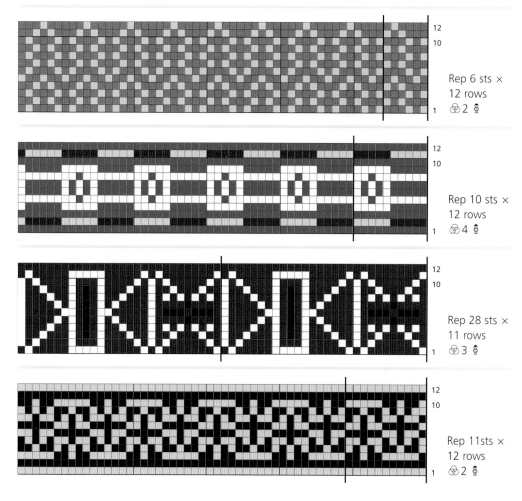

Rep 6 sts ×
12 rows
⊗2 🔥

Rep 10 sts ×
12 rows
⊗4 🔥

Rep 28 sts ×
11 rows
⊗3 🔥

Rep 11sts ×
12 rows
⊗2 🔥

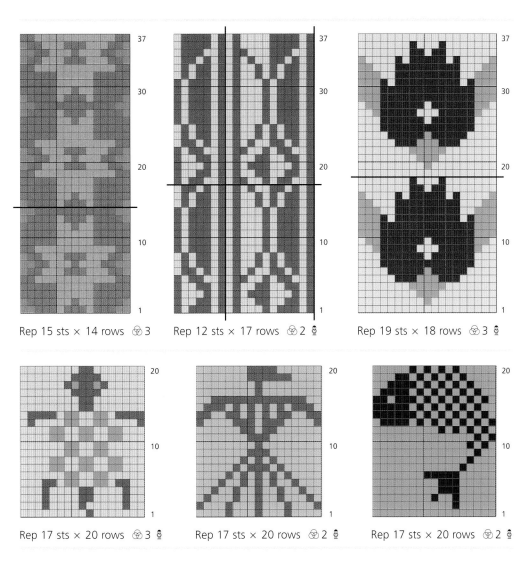

Rep 15 sts × 14 rows ⊗ 3

Rep 12 sts × 17 rows ⊗ 2 👤

Rep 19 sts × 18 rows ⊗ 3 👤

Rep 17 sts × 20 rows ⊗ 3 👤

Rep 17 sts × 20 rows ⊗ 2 👤

Rep 17 sts × 20 rows ⊗ 2 👤

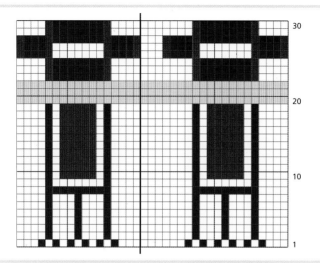

Rep 20 sts ×
30 rows
🌀 4 👤 ▷

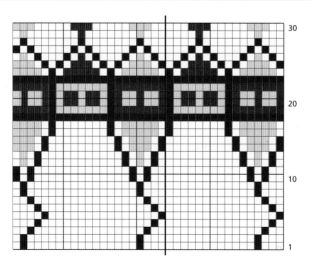

Rep 16 sts × 30
rows 🌀 4 👤 ▷

Rep 60 sts ×
65 rows
🌀 4 👤 ▷

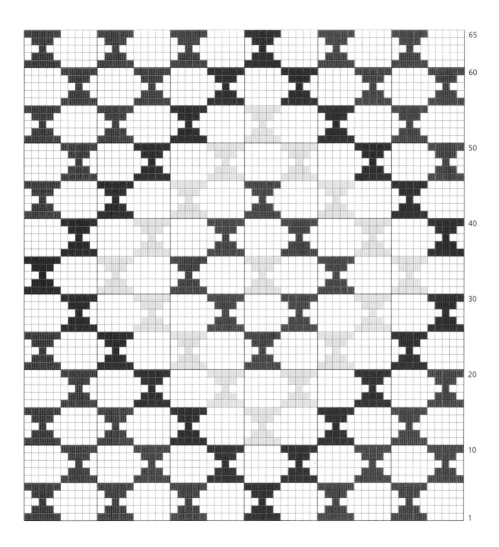

Homestead America

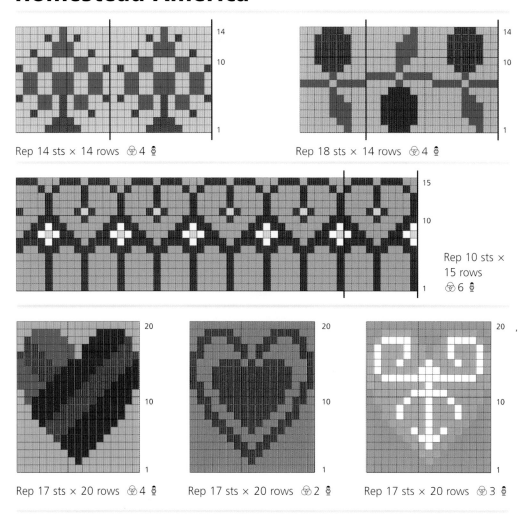

Rep 14 sts × 14 rows ⊛4 👤

Rep 18 sts × 14 rows ⊛4 👤

Rep 10 sts × 15 rows ⊛6 👤

Rep 17 sts × 20 rows ⊛4 👤

Rep 17 sts × 20 rows ⊛2 👤

Rep 17 sts × 20 rows ⊛3 👤

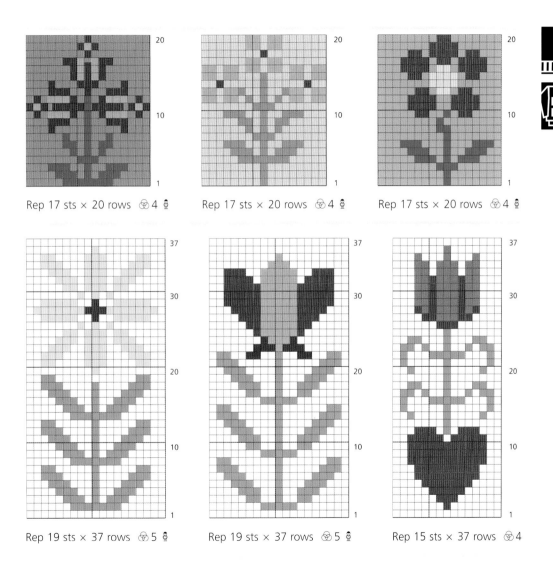

Rep 17 sts × 20 rows ⊛4 ⬤

Rep 17 sts × 20 rows ⊛4 ⬤

Rep 17 sts × 20 rows ⊛4 ⬤

Rep 19 sts × 37 rows ⊛5 ⬤

Rep 19 sts × 37 rows ⊛5 ⬤

Rep 15 sts × 37 rows ⊛4

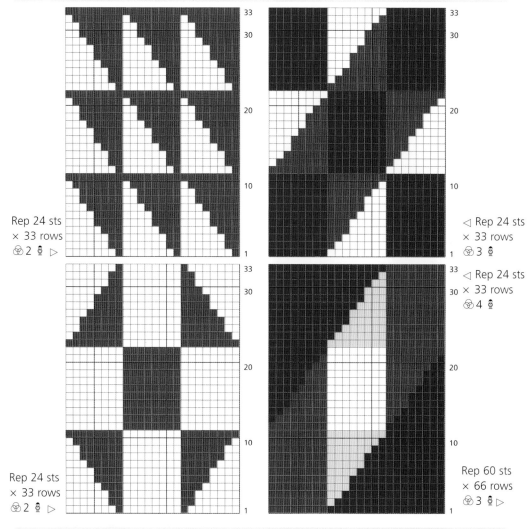

Rep 24 sts
× 33 rows
❀2 👤 ▷

◁ Rep 24 sts
× 33 rows
❀3 👤

◁ Rep 24 sts
× 33 rows
❀4 👤

Rep 24 sts
× 33 rows
❀2 👤 ▷

Rep 60 sts
× 66 rows
❀3 👤 ▷

Aztec and Inca

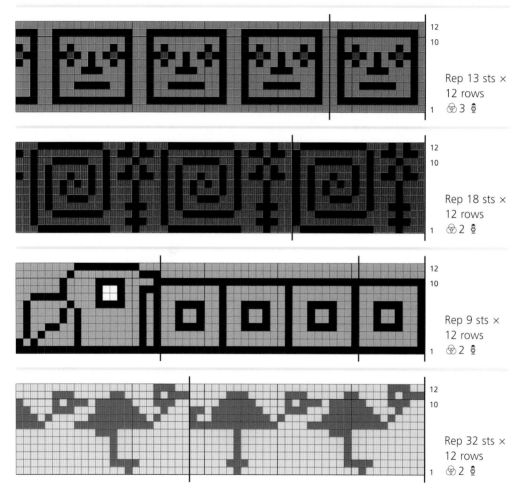

Rep 13 sts ×
12 rows

Rep 18 sts ×
12 rows

Rep 9 sts ×
12 rows

Rep 32 sts ×
12 rows

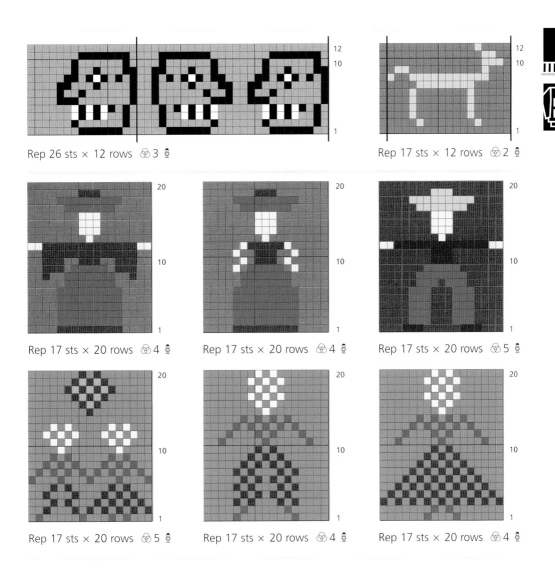

Rep 26 sts × 12 rows ⊛ 3 ⚇

Rep 17 sts × 12 rows ⊛ 2 ⚇

Rep 17 sts × 20 rows ⊛ 4 ⚇

Rep 17 sts × 20 rows ⊛ 4 ⚇

Rep 17 sts × 20 rows ⊛ 5 ⚇

Rep 17 sts × 20 rows ⊛ 5 ⚇

Rep 17 sts × 20 rows ⊛ 4 ⚇

Rep 17 sts × 20 rows ⊛ 4 ⚇

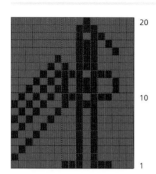

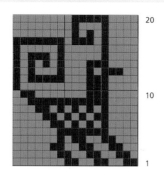

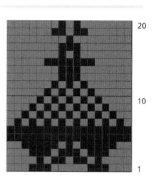

Rep 17 sts × 20 rows 2

Rep 17 sts × 20 rows 2

Rep 17 sts × 20 rows 2

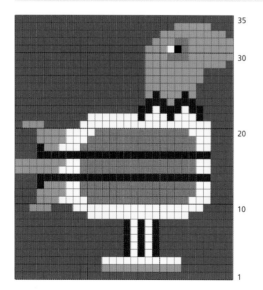

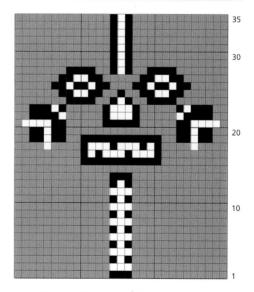

Rep 30 sts × 35 rows 6

Rep 29 sts × 35 rows 3

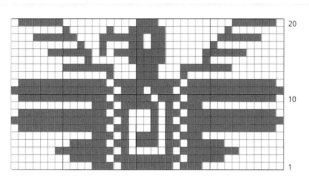

Rep 37 sts ×
20 rows
⊛2 ⚱

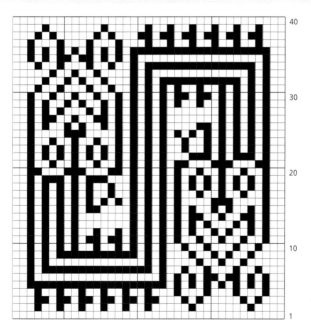

Rep 37 sts ×
40 rows
⊛2 ⚱

Celts

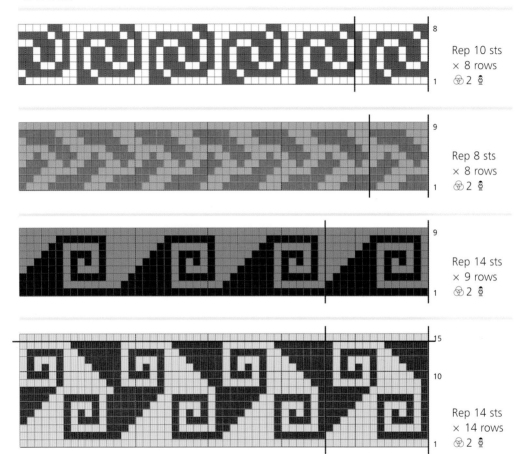

Rep 10 sts
× 8 rows
⊛2 ☗

Rep 8 sts
× 8 rows
⊛2 ☗

Rep 14 sts
× 9 rows
⊛2 ☗

Rep 14 sts
× 14 rows
⊛2 ☗

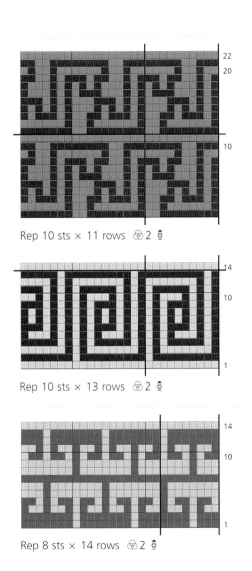

Rep 10 sts × 11 rows ⊛2 ⚇

Rep 10 sts × 13 rows ⊛2 ⚇

Rep 8 sts × 14 rows ⊛2 ⚇

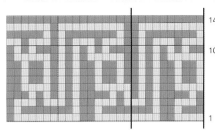
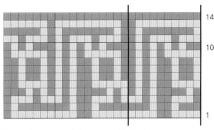
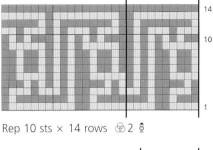

Rep 10 sts × 14 rows ⊛2 ⚇

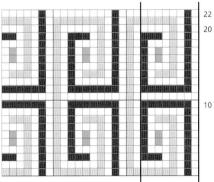

Rep 8 sts × 22 rows ⊛4

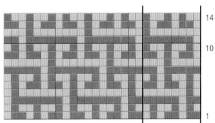

Rep 8 sts × 14 rows ⊛2 ⚇

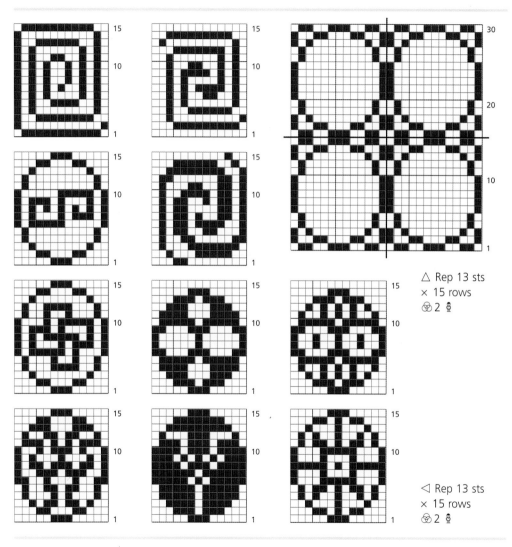

△ Rep 13 sts
× 15 rows
2

◁ Rep 13 sts
× 15 rows
2

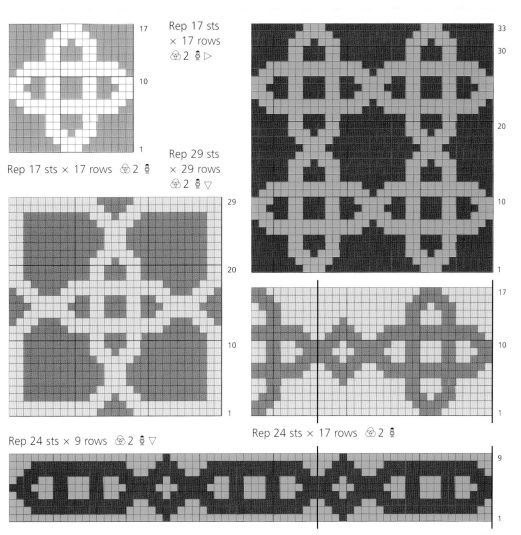

Rep 17 sts
× 17 rows
⊛ 2 ♟ ▷

Rep 29 sts
× 29 rows
⊛ 2 ♟ ▽

Rep 17 sts × 17 rows ⊛ 2 ♟

Rep 24 sts × 9 rows ⊛ 2 ♟ ▽

Rep 24 sts × 17 rows ⊛ 2 ♟

Middle East and Arab

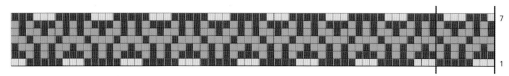

Rep 8 sts × 7 rows ⊛3 ⛫

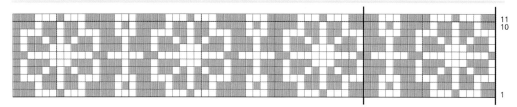

Rep 18 sts × 11 rows ⊛2 ⛫

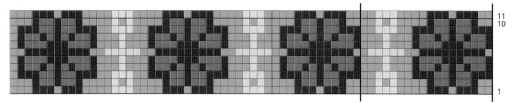

Rep 18 sts × 11 rows ⊛4

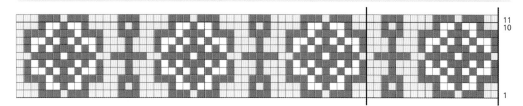

Rep 18 sts × 11 rows ⊛3 ⛫

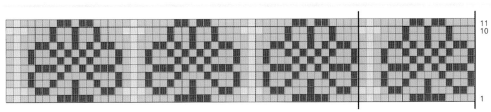

Rep 16 sts × 11 rows ⊗ 3 👤

Rep 11 sts
× 12 rows
⊗ 2 👤

Rep 14 sts
× 13 rows
⊗ 2 👤

Rep 28 sts
× 13 rows
⊗ 3 👤

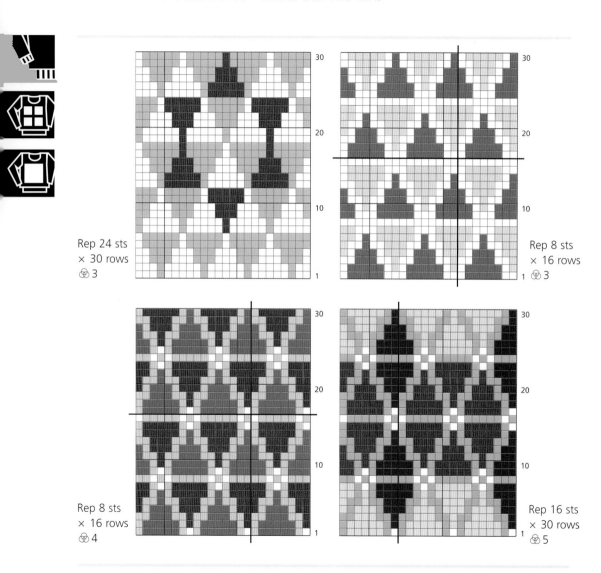

Rep 24 sts
× 30 rows
🌐 3

Rep 8 sts
× 16 rows
🌐 3

Rep 8 sts
× 16 rows
🌐 4

Rep 16 sts
× 30 rows
🌐 5

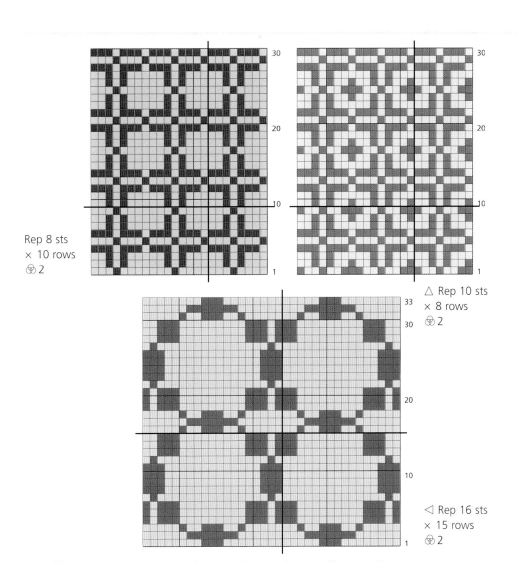

Rep 8 sts
× 10 rows
⊛ 2

△ Rep 10 sts
× 8 rows
⊛ 2

◁ Rep 16 sts
× 15 rows
⊛ 2

Africa

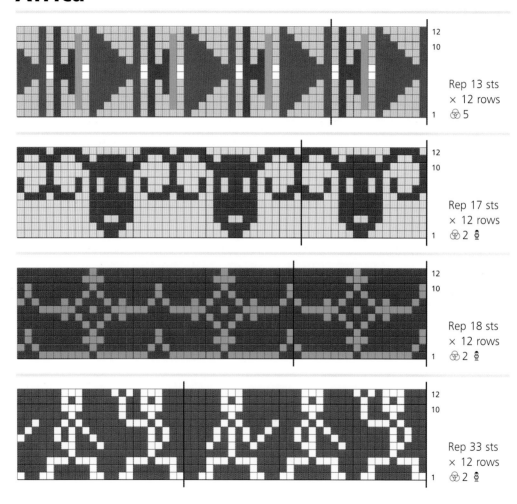

Rep 13 sts
× 12 rows
⊛ 5

Rep 17 sts
× 12 rows
⊛ 2 ⚱

Rep 18 sts
× 12 rows
⊛ 2 ⚱

Rep 33 sts
× 12 rows
⊛ 2 ⚱

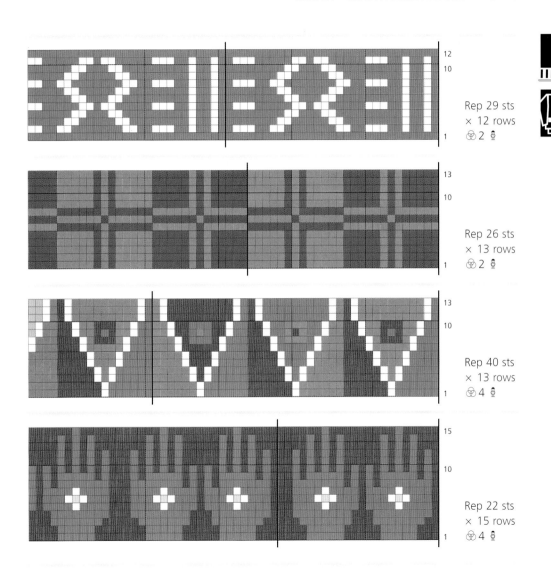

Rep 29 sts
× 12 rows
🞉2 🮲

Rep 26 sts
× 13 rows
🞉2 🮲

Rep 40 sts
× 13 rows
🞉4 🮲

Rep 22 sts
× 15 rows
🞉4 🮲

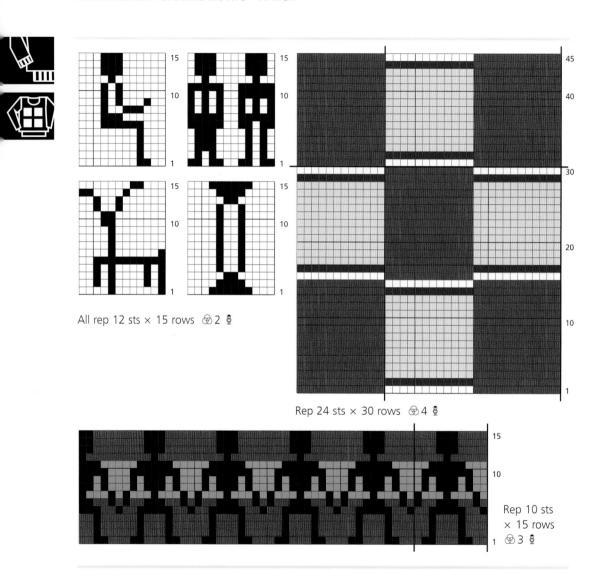

All rep 12 sts × 15 rows ⊛2 ⚉

Rep 24 sts × 30 rows ⊛4 ⚉

Rep 10 sts
× 15 rows
⊛3 ⚉

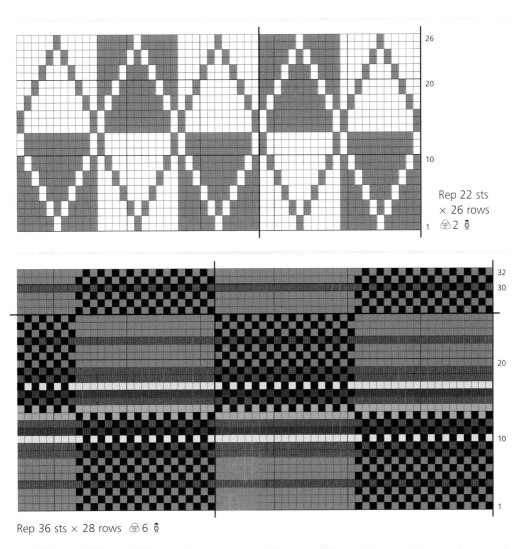

Rep 22 sts
× 26 rows
⊛ 2 ⚲

Rep 36 sts × 28 rows ⊛ 6 ⚲

India and Tibet

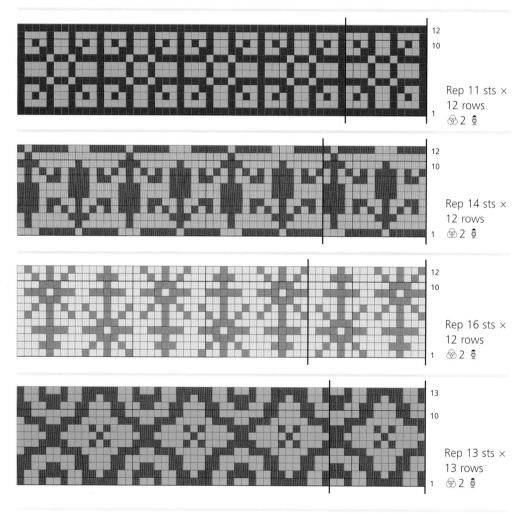

Rep 11 sts ×
12 rows

Rep 14 sts ×
12 rows

Rep 16 sts ×
12 rows

Rep 13 sts ×
13 rows

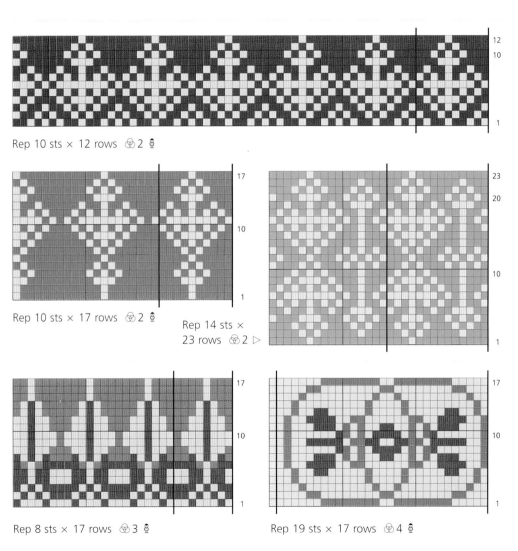

Rep 10 sts × 12 rows ⊛2 ⏾

Rep 10 sts × 17 rows ⊛2 ⏾

Rep 14 sts ×
23 rows ⊛2 ▷

Rep 8 sts × 17 rows ⊛3 ⏾

Rep 19 sts × 17 rows ⊛4 ⏾

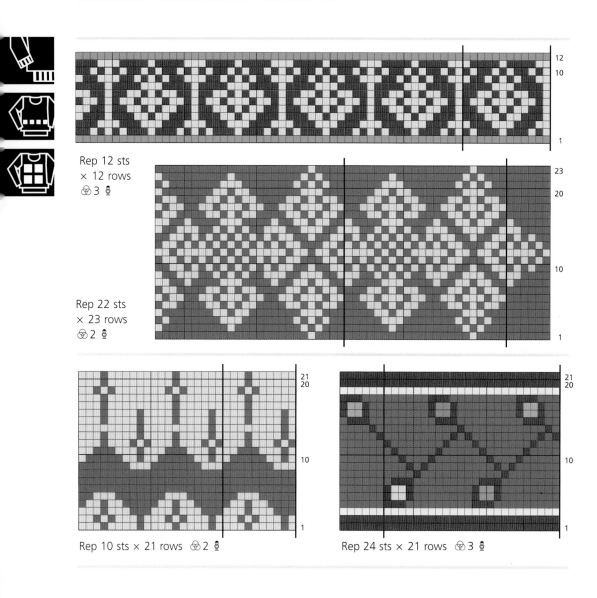

Rep 12 sts
× 12 rows
⊛3 👤

Rep 22 sts
× 23 rows
⊛2 👤

Rep 10 sts × 21 rows ⊛2 👤

Rep 24 sts × 21 rows ⊛3 👤

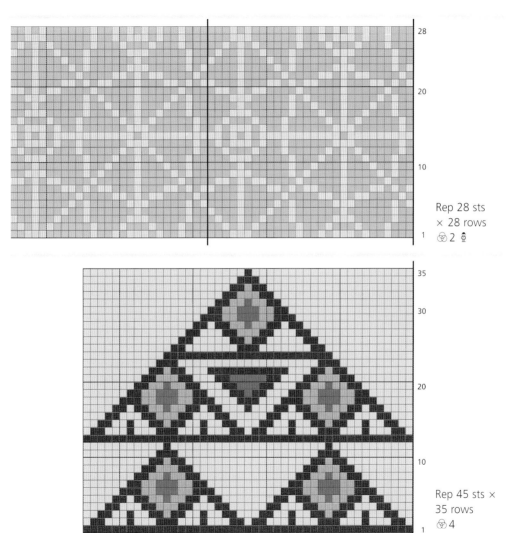

Rep 28 sts
× 28 rows

Rep 45 sts ×
35 rows

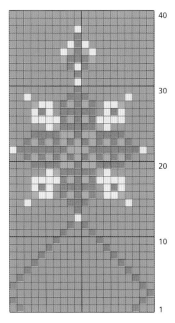

Rep 20 sts × 38 rows ✿ 4

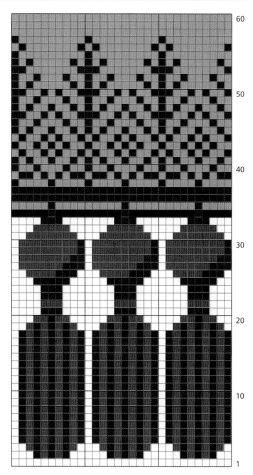

Rep 30 sts × 60 rows ✿ 5

Modern
pictorial motifs

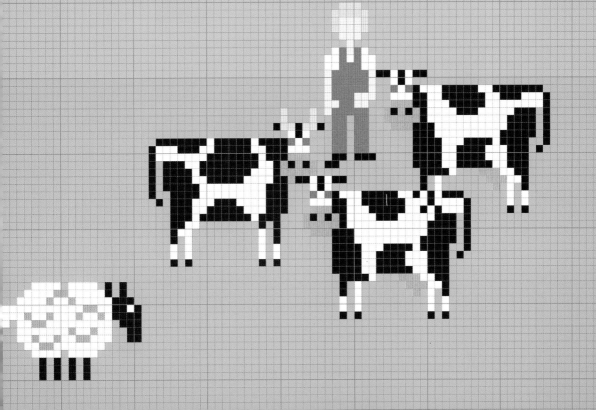

Alphabet

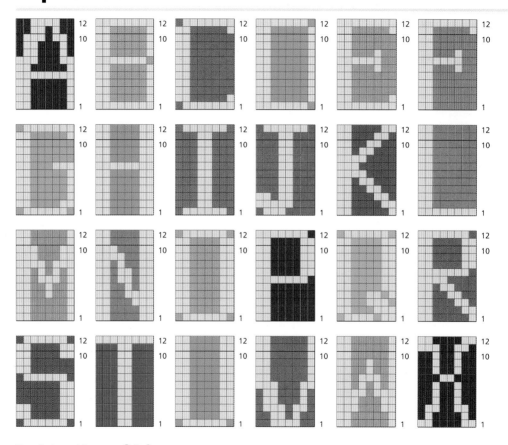

Rep 8 sts × 12 rows ⊛2 ♨ △ ▷

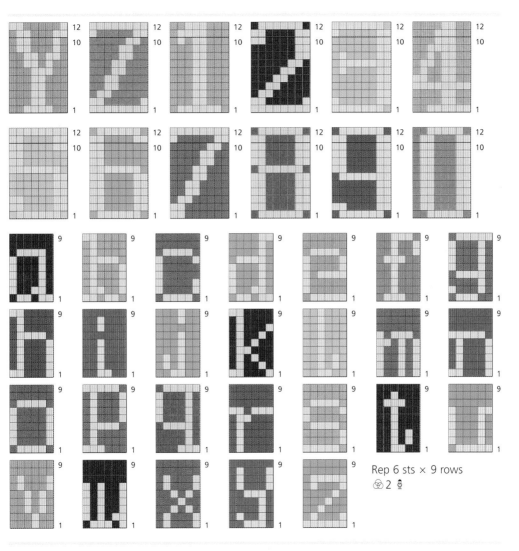

Rep 6 sts × 9 rows

Zodiac

Aries

Taurus

Gemini

Cancer

Leo

Virgo

Libra

Scorpio

Sagittarius

Capricorn

Aquarius

Pisces

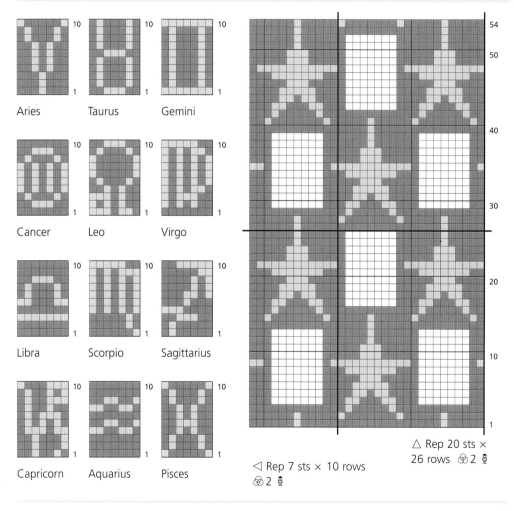

◁ Rep 7 sts × 10 rows
⊛ 2 👤

△ Rep 20 sts ×
26 rows ⊛ 2 👤

The world around us

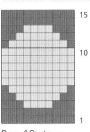

Rep 10 sts ×
15 rows ⊛2 ⚇

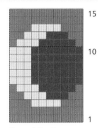

Rep 10 sts ×
15 rows ⊛3 ⚇

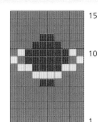

Rep 10 sts ×
15 rows ⊛3 ⚇

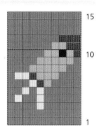

Rep 10 sts ×
15 rows ⊛5 ⚇

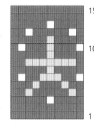

Rep 10 sts ×
15 rows ⊛3 ⚇

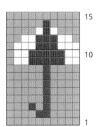

Rep 10 sts ×
15 rows ⊛4 ⚇

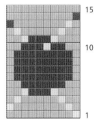

Rep 10 sts ×
15 rows ⊛4 ⚇

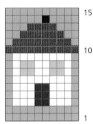

Rep 10 sts ×
15 rows ⊛5 ⚇

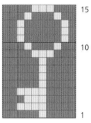

Rep 10 sts ×
15 rows ⊛2 ⚇

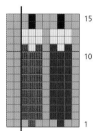

Rep 10 sts ×
15 rows ⊛5 ⚇

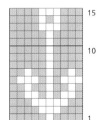

Rep 10 sts ×
15 rows ⊛2 ⚇

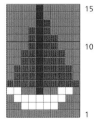

Rep 10 sts ×
15 rows ⊛4 ⚇

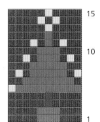

Rep 10 sts ×
15 rows ⊛5 ⚇

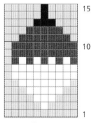

Rep 10 sts ×
15 rows ⊛4 ⚇

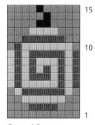

Rep 10 sts ×
15 rows ⊛4 ⚇

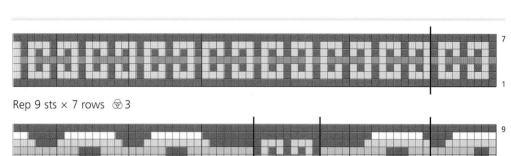

Rep 9 sts × 7 rows ⊛3

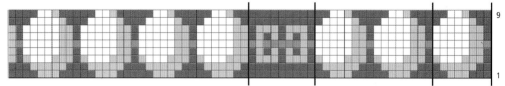

Rep 15 sts + 9 sts × 7 rows ⊛6

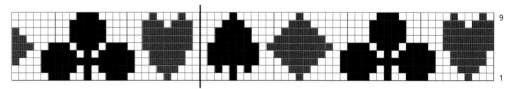

Rep 8 sts + 9 sts × 7 rows ⊛4

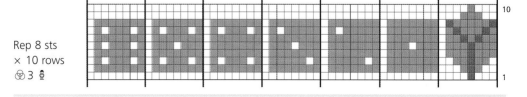

Rep 40 sts × 9 rows ⊛3 ⌰

Rep 8 sts
× 10 rows
⊛3 ⌰

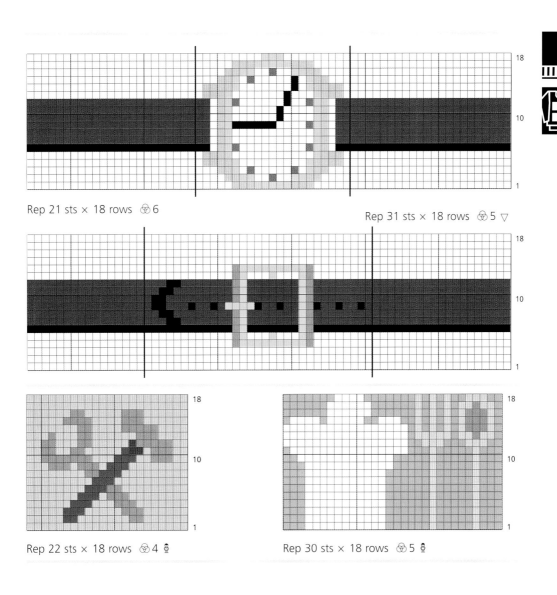

Rep 21 sts × 18 rows ⊛6

Rep 31 sts × 18 rows ⊛5 ▽

Rep 22 sts × 18 rows ⊛4 🕴

Rep 30 sts × 18 rows ⊛5 🕴

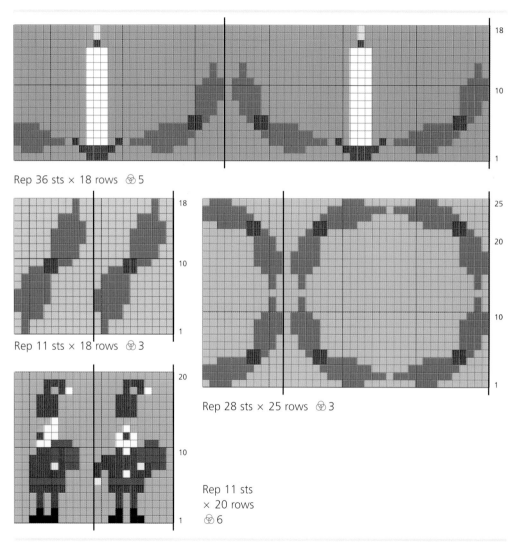

Rep 36 sts × 18 rows ⊛ 5

Rep 11 sts × 18 rows ⊛ 3

Rep 28 sts × 25 rows ⊛ 3

Rep 11 sts
× 20 rows
⊛ 6

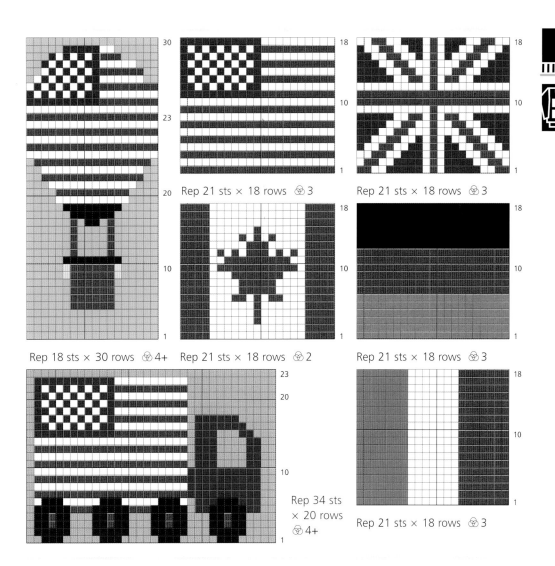

Rep 18 sts × 30 rows ⊛ 4+

Rep 21 sts × 18 rows ⊛ 3

Rep 21 sts × 18 rows ⊛ 3

Rep 21 sts × 18 rows ⊛ 2

Rep 21 sts × 18 rows ⊛ 3

Rep 34 sts × 20 rows ⊛ 4+

Rep 21 sts × 18 rows ⊛ 3

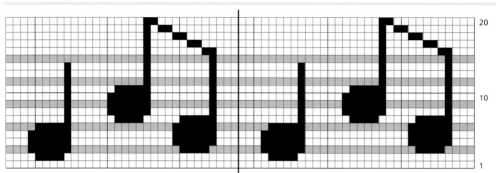

Rep 32 sts × 20 rows ⊛ 3

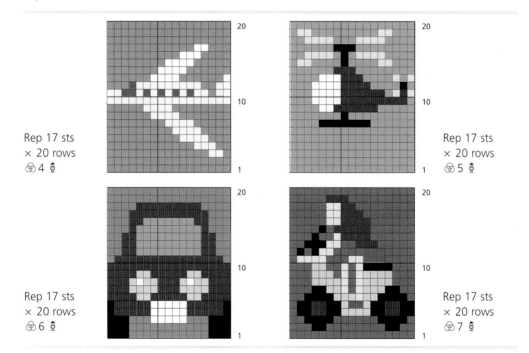

Rep 17 sts
× 20 rows
⊛ 4 🏮

Rep 17 sts
× 20 rows
⊛ 5 🏮

Rep 17 sts
× 20 rows
⊛ 6 🏮

Rep 17 sts
× 20 rows
⊛ 7 🏮

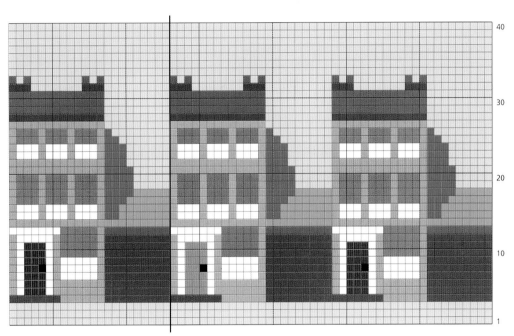

Rep 44 sts × 33 rows ✿ 12

Animals, birds and insects

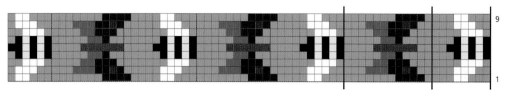

Rep 8 sts + 12 sts × 9 rows ⊛ 8 ⚱

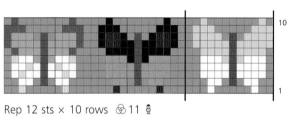

Rep 12 sts × 10 rows ⊛ 11 ⚱

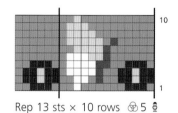

Rep 13 sts × 10 rows ⊛ 5 ⚱

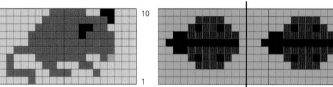

Rep 22 sts × 10 rows ⊛ 5 ⚱   Rep 13 sts × 10 rows ⊛ 3 ⚱

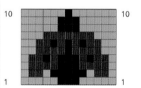

Rep 13 sts × 10 rows ⊛ 3 ⚱

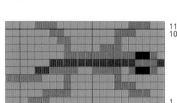

Rep 22 sts × 11 rows ⊛ 4 ⚱

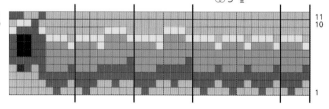

Rep 4 sts + 8 sts + 9 sts × 11 rows ⊛ 6 ⚱

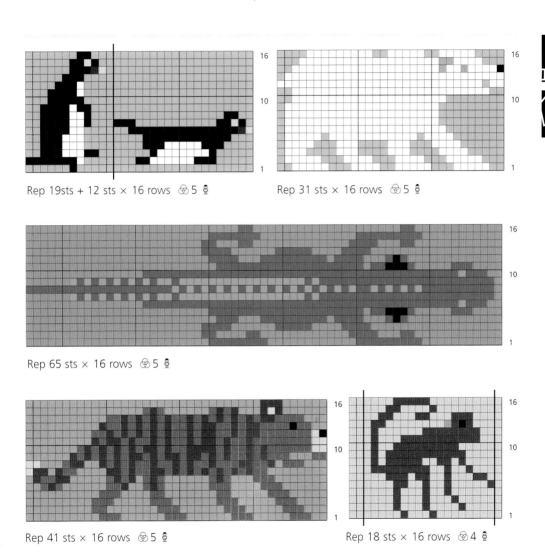

Rep 19sts + 12 sts × 16 rows ⊛5 ⚇

Rep 31 sts × 16 rows ⊛5 ⚇

Rep 65 sts × 16 rows ⊛5 ⚇

Rep 41 sts × 16 rows ⊛5 ⚇

Rep 18 sts × 16 rows ⊛4 ⚇

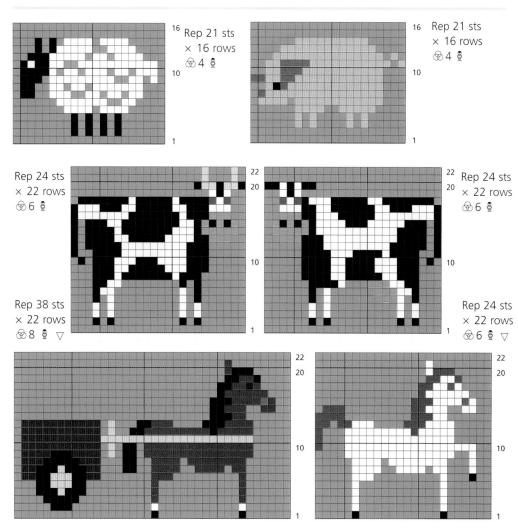

16 Rep 21 sts
× 16 rows
⊛ 4 ▯

16 Rep 21 sts
× 16 rows
⊛ 4 ▯

Rep 24 sts
× 22 rows
⊛ 6 ▯

Rep 24 sts
× 22 rows
⊛ 6 ▯

Rep 38 sts
× 22 rows
⊛ 8 ▯ ▽

Rep 24 sts
× 22 rows
⊛ 6 ▯ ▽

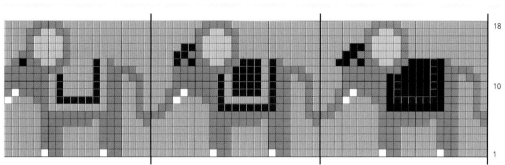

Rep 23 sts × 18 rows ⊛8 ⬩

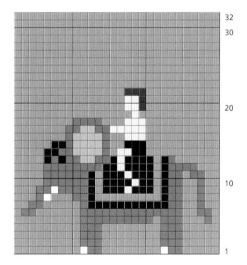

Rep 28 sts × 24 rows ⊛8 ⬩

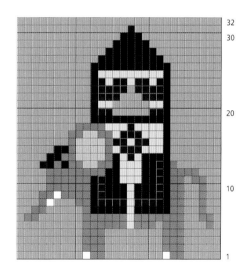

Rep 28 sts × 32 rows ⊛7 ⬩

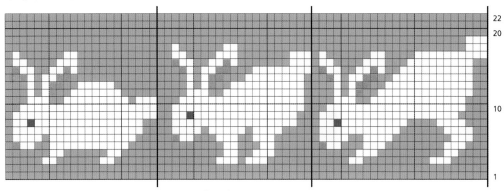

Rep 21 sts + 21 sts + 24 sts × 22 rows ⊛4 ⏳

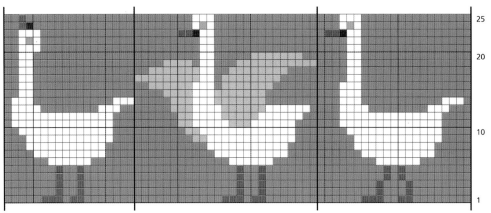

Rep 18 sts + 25 sts + 21 sts × 10 rows ⊛6 ⏳

Rep 29 sts × 25 rows ⊛ 5 ☕

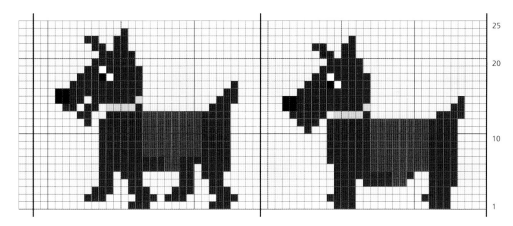

Rep 31 sts + 31 sts × 25 rows ⊛ 5 ☕

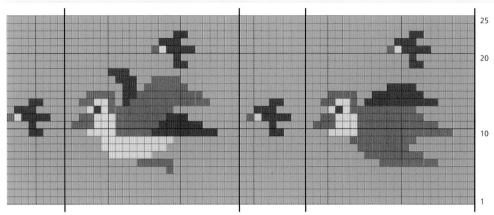

Rep 24 sts + 9 sts + 23 sts × 25 rows ⊛ 4 ☗

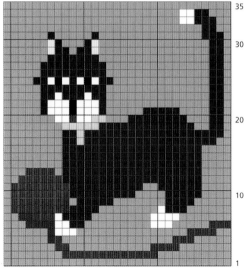

Rep 31 sts
× 35 rows
⊛ 8 ☗

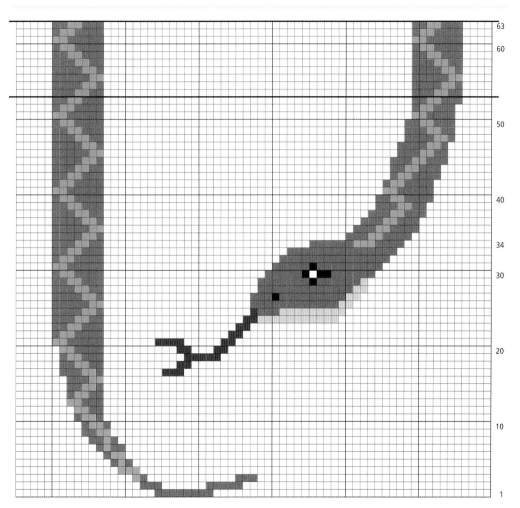

Rep 65 sts × 63 rows ⊛7 🎨 + Rep 10 rows for the body

Floral

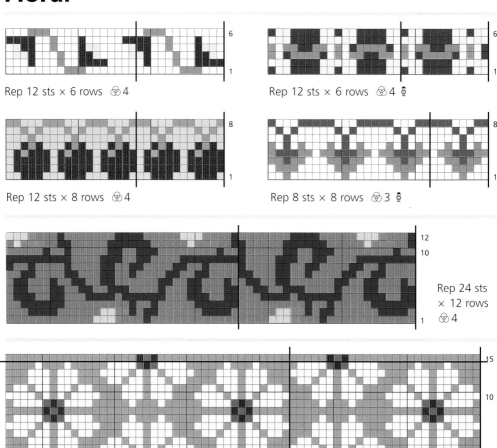

Rep 12 sts × 6 rows ✿ 4

Rep 12 sts × 6 rows ✿ 4 ⚇

Rep 12 sts × 8 rows ✿ 4

Rep 8 sts × 8 rows ✿ 3 ⚇

Rep 24 sts × 12 rows ✿ 4

Rep 26 sts × 14 rows ✿ 4

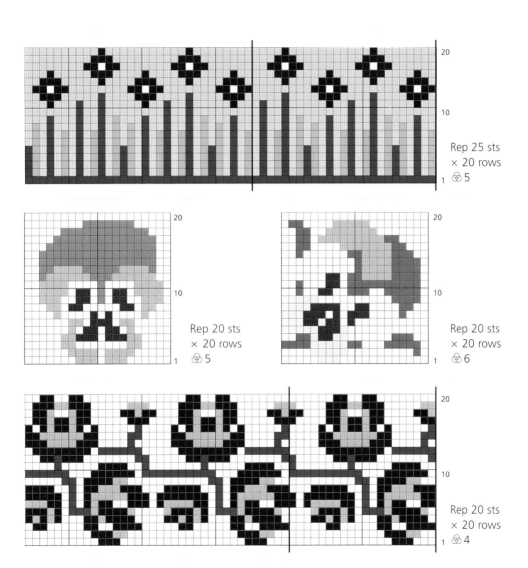

Rep 25 sts
× 20 rows
⊛ 5

Rep 20 sts
× 20 rows
⊛ 5

Rep 20 sts
× 20 rows
⊛ 6

Rep 20 sts
× 20 rows
⊛ 4

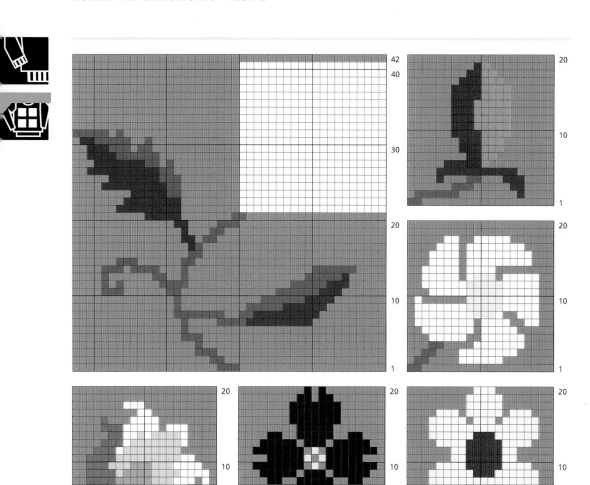

Rep 20 sts × 20 rows

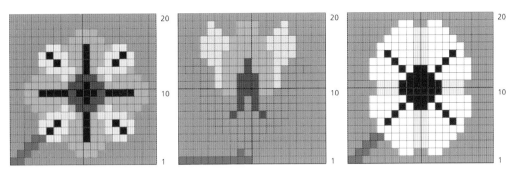

Rep 20 sts × 20 rows

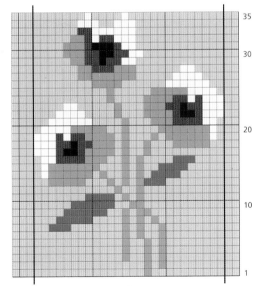

Rep 26 sts × 35 rows ⊛ 7

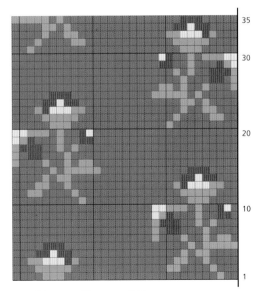

Rep 31 sts × 43 rows ⊛ 5

Toys and the nursery

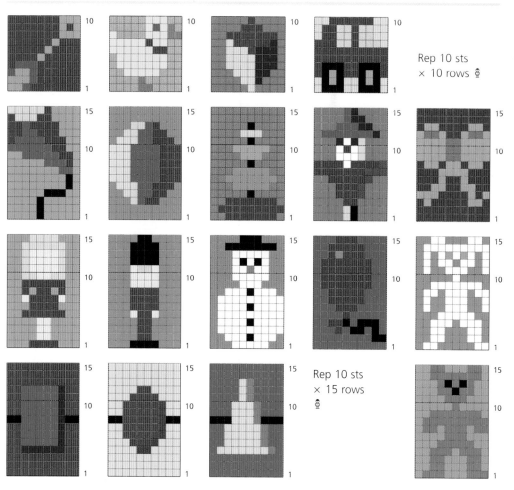

Rep 10 sts
× 10 rows

Rep 10 sts
× 15 rows

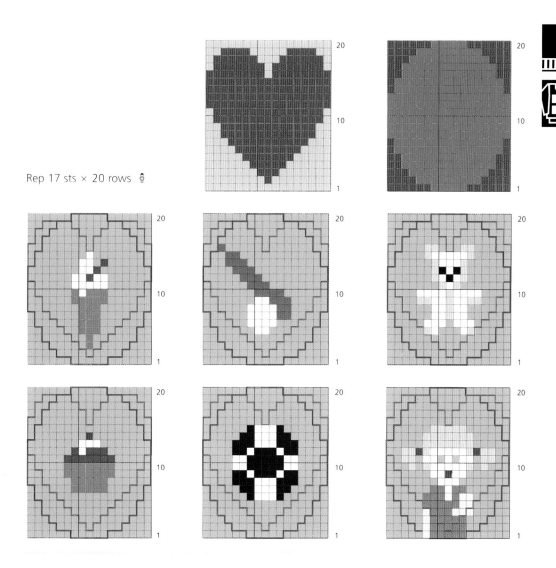

Rep 17 sts × 20 rows

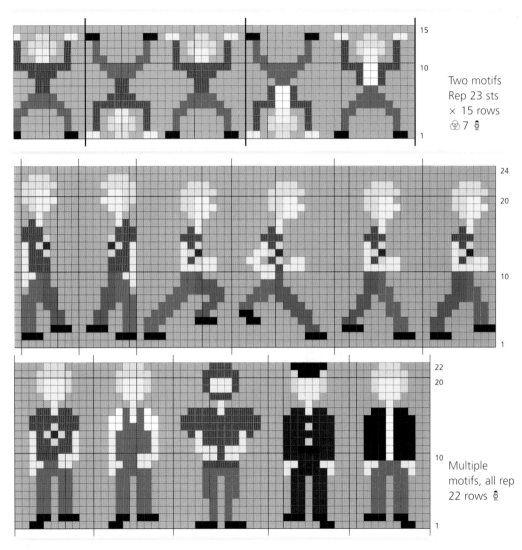

Two motifs
Rep 23 sts
× 15 rows
⊛7 ⚱

Multiple
motifs, all rep
22 rows ⚱

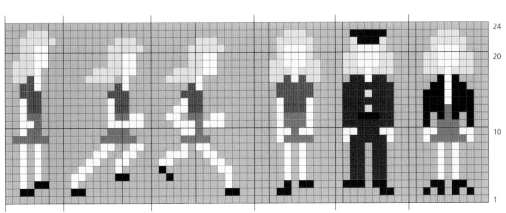

Multiple motifs, rep 22 rows 🮲

Rep 20 sts + 18 sts + 10 sts
× 23 rows ⊛8 🮲

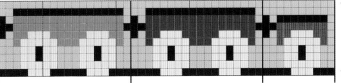

Rep 18 sts + 10 sts ×
23 rows ⊛6 🮲

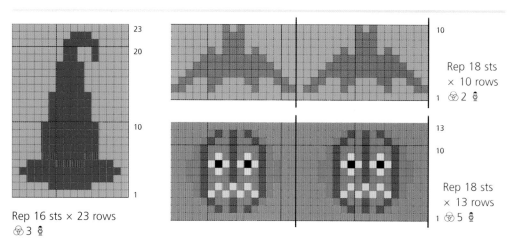

Rep 16 sts × 23 rows

Rep 18 sts × 10 rows

Rep 18 sts × 13 rows

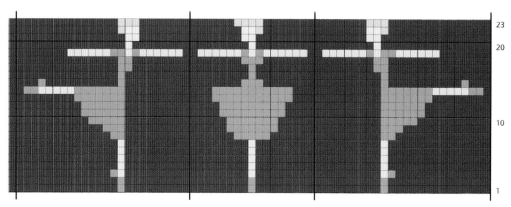

Rep 24 sts + 17 sts + 22 sts × 23 rows

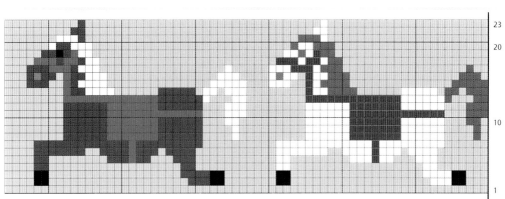

Rep 66 sts × 23 rows ⊛ 10 🯁

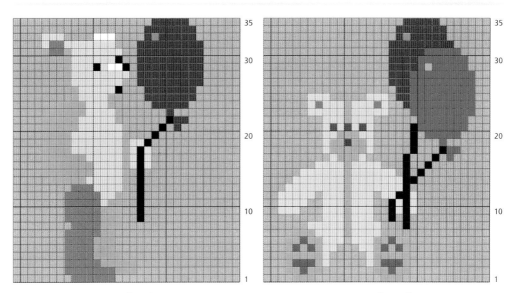

Rep 31 sts × 35 rows ⊛ 7 🯁   Rep 31 sts × 35 rows ⊛ 10 🯁

Techniques

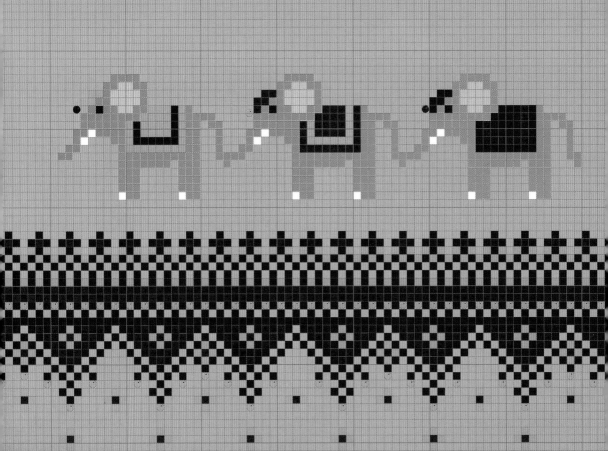

The graphs in this book can be interpreted in a variety of ways as demonstrated on pages 8–16. One of two color knitting techniques is required; Intarsia, which is used when changes of color are confined to blocks and Fair Isle, when two or more colors are used repeatedly across a row.

If a design has areas of color that are only a few stitches it may be easier and neater to embroider them using a duplicate stitch (Swiss darning).

Intarsia

Intarsia is a technique used for color knitting, when color forms distinct blocks within a design and separate lengths of yarn are used for each area of color. As the colors used on a motif are not carried across the row, a single weight of fabric is created and less yarn is used. However, where the two colors meet, the two yarns must be twisted together to avoid creating a hole.

Winding a bobbin

There can be several color changes along a row. Each block of color has a length of yarn, which is wound round a bobbin to prevent the yarn tangling. Bobbins can either be shaped plastic, manufactured for the purpose, or small pieces of card with notches cut into the edges to stop the yarn unravelling uncontrollably. Short lengths of yarn can then be unwound and secured again as required.

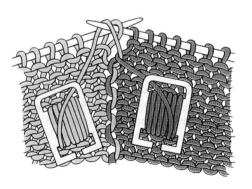

To calculate the amount of yarn required for each bobbin, use the graph to count the number of stitches to be worked in that color, then calculate how many rows that represents on the gauge (tension) swatch knitted for the project. Draw yarn from the ball or hank four times across the width of the gauge (tension) swatch for each of the rows the number of stitches on the graph represents, and cut the yarn. Then, starting with the end just cut and wind the yarn onto a bobbin.

Joining in a new color

Different colored yarns are often introduced into the design in the middle of the row. For a secure start, insert the right needle into the next stitch, rest the tail of the new color across the right needle, and then under and over the old color before knitting the next stitch in the new color. Proceed with the new color allowing its tail to fall to the back of the work. This tail

can either be darned in at the end or woven behind the following stitches using the weaving technique on page 283.

Twisting two colors together

With Intarsia knitting, it is always important to twist the two yarns at a color change together on the wrong side of the work. This prevents holes and effectively joins the two areas of color knitting.

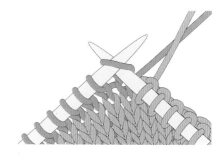

On a knit row

Knit the last stitch in the old color, drop the yarn and pick up the new color by reaching under the old color. This ensures that the new color loops around the old color before it is knitted and the two yarns are twisted together. Knit the first stitch in the new color firmly for a neat edge.

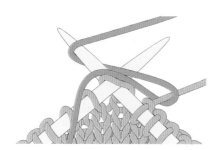

On a purl row

Purl the last stitch in the old color, lay it across
the new yarn and pick up the new color to be
purled. The new color loops around the old
color before the next stitch is purled and the
two edges are drawn together.

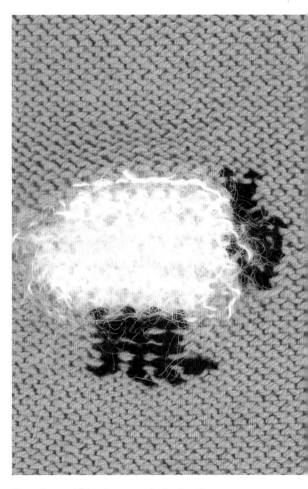

*Here the motif has been worked using the
Intarsia technique, and the yarn ends sewn
in following the outline of the shape and
yarn change.*

Fair Isle knitting

Fair Isle knitting can be approached in two different ways depending on the distance between the color changes in a row.

If the color changes are no more than four to five stitches apart then stranding can be used but if the distances are more, then it is better if the yarn is periodically woven into the fabric in a way that it does not show on the front. They are not mutually exclusive and both techniques can be used, as appropriate, across a row or design. Fair Isle knitting creates a double thickness of fabric and has a reduced elasticity compared to one color or Intarsia knitting. Fair Isle knitting also has added warmth and strength.

Stranding

If the distances between color changes are not too great then the yarn that is not being used can be left at the back of the work until it is required; then it is simply knitted or purled in the usual way. This creates a series of loops or "floats" at the back of the work.

On a knit row
Knit the last stitch in the old color, pick up the new color and without pulling too tight and creating a tuck running vertically, knit the next stitch in the new color. The yarns don't need to be twisted together.

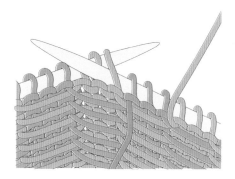

On a purl row
Purl the last stitch in the old color, pick up the new color and purl the next stitch in the new color. The float at the back of the work should have a slight droop from the horizontal to retain some of the elasticity of knitting.

Weaving

If the distance between color changes is more than five stitches then weaving is used to secure potentially long floats. If these loops are not secured they can catch and pull, distorting the evenness of the work.

Do not be tempted to weave in a potentially long float every other stitch. It will look neater on the wrong side but it will dramatically change the drape of the fabric. After all, this technique is often used to strengthen the heels of socks and the elbows of sweaters that can expect heavy wear.

The following illustrations show step-by-step how to weave in a yarn, however the actual design would work better using the Intarsia technique; it has only been used here to illustrate the point. The working yarn is the yarn that will create the stitch and appear at the front.

On a knit row

Insert the right needle into the next stitch as if to knit.

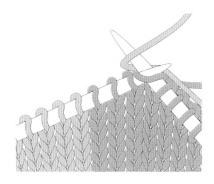

Pick up the color to be woven in and without pulling too tight, wrap it round the right needle as if to knit.

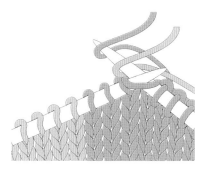

Wrap the working yarn around the needle in the same way but before drawing the loop through to create the stitch, take the yarn to be woven back round the needle in a counter-clockwise direction.

On a purl row

The working yarn is the yarn that will create
the stitch and appear at the front. Insert the
right needle into the next stitch as if to purl.

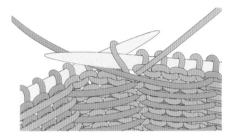

Pick up the color to be woven in and without
pulling too tight, loop it under the right needle.

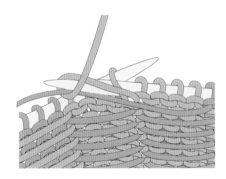

Wrap the working yarn around the needle as if
to purl but before drawing the loop through to
create the stitch, bring the yarn to be woven
in down toward the base of the work and back
round the needle in a counter-clockwise
direction.

Knitting stripes back and forth

Some motifs demand that a color is used in
bands within a design. If the number of rows
between each band is an even number then
the yarn need not be cut but can be picked up
and used as required. If the distance between
the bands of color is more than six rows it is
useful to weave in the yarn not in use every
few rows, two stitches from the edge. This
secures the potentially long vertical float.

  If you are knitting a stripe pattern that has
uneven rows between a color stripe, then
rather than breaking off and rejoining the yarn,
use double-pointed or circular needles. If the
yarn is at the other end of the work, pick up
the yarn and work as the pattern set from the
opposite end. This may mean that if the
pattern is stockinette (stocking) stitch, two
rows of either purl or knit stitches are worked
but the pattern will be correct.

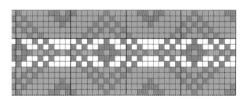

Tip

For some patterns it is useful to find and knit
from both ends of the yarn. Alternatively, wind
half the yarn into a second ball and start
knitting from the center of the ball, using
either of the two ends as required.

Duplicate stitch (Swiss darning)

This embroidery stitch duplicates the look of a knit stitch and is added to a knitted surface after the knitting is finished. This technique can be used for small, isolated, patches of color of only one to four stitches which would be difficult to knit neatly using one of the other techniques described. However, even if the tension of the knitted fabric is followed carefully it is difficult to make it look convincing as a knitted stitch over large solid areas. Large solid areas are easier and quicker to knit. Duplicate stitch (Swiss darning) is a good way of using up small scraps of yarn.

Vertically
Work from bottom to top. Thread a tapestry needle, leaving a long tail. Bring the needle up from the back to the front of the work through the base of the first stitch. Follow the knitted stitch behind the stitch above and then insert the needle back through the base of the same stitch and up through the base of the stitch above. Continue in this way as required.

Finishing
Before securing the ends ease the stitches and ensure the tension matches that of the knitted fabric.

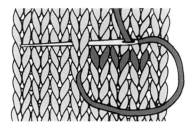

Horizontally
Work from right to left. Thread a tapestry needle, leaving a long tail. Bring the needle up from the back to the front of the work through the base of a stitch Follow the knitted stitch behind the stitch above and then insert the needle back through the base of the same stitch and up through the base of the stitch to the left. Continue in this way along the row as required.

Abbreviations

beg	beginning/begin
C4B	cable 4 back. Slip the next 2 sts onto a cable needle and hold at the back of the work. Knit 2 sts from the left needle and then the 2 sts from the cable needle. The number in the center can vary, see pattern instructions for more details.
C4F	cable 4 front. Slip the next 2 sts onto a cable needle and hold at the front of the work. Knit 2 sts from the left needle and then the 2 sts from the cable needle. The number in the center can vary, see pattern instructions for more details.
col	color/colorway
cont	continue
cm	centimeter
dec	decrease
dp	double pointed
foll	following
folls	follows
g	grams
in	inch
inc	increase
k	knit

k2tog	knit 2 stitches together.
mb	make bobble small: (k1, p1) twice into the same stitch, turn and p4, turn and sl2, k2tog, p2sso. make bobble medium: (k1, p1) twice into the same stitch, turn and p4, turn k4, turn p4 turn and sl2, k2tog, p2sso. make bobble large: (k1, p1) three times into the same stitch, pass each new stitch over the first stitch and off the needle. make bobble large alt: (k1, p1) three times into the same stitch, turn and p6, turn and sl3, k3tog, p3sso.
ml	make loop: K next st leaving st on left needle, bring yarn forward between needles, wrap the yarn round thumb of left-hand to make a loop, take yarn between needles to back of work and K same st again, slipping st off left needle. Slip the the stitches just made back onto the left needle and knit two together.
mm	millimeter
m1	make one stitch.
oz	ounces
p	purl
patt	pattern
pb	place bead: thread beads onto yarn before starting to knit each section: (RS): with yarn forward, slide bead up

yarn, slip 1 stitch purlwise, yarn back leaving bead in front of the slipped stitch.

(WS): with yarn back, slide bead up yarn, slip 1 stitch purlwise, yarn forward leaving bead in front of slipped stitch.

psso	pass slipped stitch over.
p2sso	pass the 2 slipped stitches over.
p3sso	pass the 3 slipped stitches over.
p2tog	purl 2 stitches together.
rep	repeat
reps	repeats
RS	right side of work
sl	slip
st/sts	stitch/stitches
WS	wrong side of work.
yb	yarn back
yf	yarn forward
yo	yarn forward and over needle to make a stitch.
*	repeat instructions between * as many times as instructed.
[ ]	repeat instructions between [ ] as many times as instructed.

Conversions

Needle sizes

US SIZE	METRIC SIZE	OLD UK & CANADIAN SIZE
15	10	000
13	9	00
11	8	0
11	7½	1
10½	7	2
10½	6½	3
10	6	4
9	5½	5
8	5	6
7	4½	7
6	4	8
5	3¾	9
4	3½	–
3	3¼	10
2/3	3	11
2	2¾	12
1	2¼	13
0	2	14

Weights and lengths

oz	=	g × 0.0352
g	=	oz × 28.35
in	=	cm × 0.3937
cm	=	in × 2.54
yd	=	m × 0.9144
m	=	yd × 1.0936

Acknowledgments

As always, this book has been a team effort with an army of people, not always acknowledged, playing key roles and working long hours beyond the call of duty to get it on the shelves.
I hope you are not disappointed and I thank and appreciate you all.

I would like to extend special thanks to Kuo Kang Chen, without whose illustrative talents and patience this book would not exist. Thank you!

Suppliers

Every project will look better if knitted with good quality yarns. In this book, Rowan Yarns and Jaeger Handknits have been used.

Suppliers of Rowan Yarns and Jaeger Handknits

USA
Westminster Fibers, Inc.
4 Townsend West, Suite 8
Nashua, NH 03063
Tel: 603 886 5041
Fax: 603 886 1056
www.knitrowan.com

Australia
Rowan at Sunspun
185 Canterbury Road
Canterbury
Victoria 3126
Tel: 03 9830 1609

Canada
Diamond Yarn
9697 St Laurent
Montreal
Quebec H3L 2N1
Tel: 514 388 6188

Diamond Yarn (Toronto)
155 Martin Ross
Unit 3
Toronto
Ontario M3J 2L9
Tel: 416 736 6111

UK
Rowan Yarns and Jaeger
Handknits
Green Lane Mill
Holmfirth
West Yorkshire
HD9 2DX
Tel: 01484 681881
www.knitrowan.com